No Longer a Slave

How to Break the Chains of Sin and Bondage

No Longer a Slave: How to Break the Chains of Sin and Bondage

Trilogy Christian Publishers A Wholly Owned Subsidiary of Trinity Broadcasting Network

2442 Michelle Drive Tustin, CA 92780

Manufactured in the United States of America

10 9 8 7 6 5 4 3 2 1

Library of Congress Cataloging-in-Publication Data is available.

ISBN: 978-1-64773-620-0

E-ISBN: 978-1-64773-621-7

Dedication

I dedicate this book to my Lord and Savior, Jesus Christ. He is the one who has many names throughout the world ranging from Jehovah-Jireh to Yahweh. You never left me or abandoned me. You loved me in spite of my flaws. You saved me, and You believed in me when no one else would. Heavenly Father, You gave Your Son, who then shed His blood so that sinners like me could know You personally and speak to You one on one. I thank You for Your grace and Your mercy, which is sufficient to cover all my sins. I pray this book touches the lives of millions, and I pray the proceeds bring resources to Your kingdom in places that need it the most.

To my wife and best friend, Kayla. Thank you for believing in me and remaining by my side consistently, without fail. Your love is like a flame that burned during the coldest hours of my life. That flame kept my heart from going cold, and God used you as the light which led me back to Him. I will be forever grateful for every second you give me. You motivate and inspire me constantly to become the man that God has called me to be. I still adore you.

To my daughter in heaven, Allazha. May your presence forever rest with me, and may your memories never fade from my mind. Allandra, my first born, I have not always been the perfect father. For that, I'm sorry, but I love you now more than ever. God is going to use you in ways that you can't even imagine. I'm proud to be your dad and even prouder of the young woman you are becoming. Allandis Jr., my son, I love you so much, and I thank God for making you better than me in so many ways. You are intelligent and outspoken. Your gifts will help this world become a better place. I'm proud of you also, son.

Carson, you are an entrepreneur and natural born leader. I see God using you in great ways. You are truly special in many ways. Elliot, I have never met a young man with a heart as pure as yours.

Surely God's hand is upon you. I can't wait to witness His works in you. Max, you are a walking miracle. Your story has already inspired many, and the best is yet to come. You bring joy to many including me. Quinn, our angel. God has set you apart for a special purpose. You are so beautiful yet so full of love. I love you all, and I thank God for the privilege of being in your lives.

To my mother, LeDante. You have spoken over my life since I was a baby. Your prayers have covered me during my rebellion, and your love never failed me. Thank you for all the sacrifices that you made for us! Now it's your time to shine. May God bless every book that you publish. You are a blessing to the body of Christ. I love you momma.

To my Pastors, Jerome Trott Sr. and Steven White. Thank you for being true examples of what a man of God looks like. I respect and admire you both. May God continuously bless Kingdom Life Ministries and Life Church.

TABLE OF CONTENTS

Intro

You are bound by weights that you can't see. You feel as though you are chained like an animal or a slave but have no idea how to break free. You have carried this weight for as long as you can remember, and you're tired of living this way. There has to be a way to break free! But *how*?

"How do I break free of the emotions, drugs, lies, and lifestyle that has me bound?" You ask yourself. By the end of this book, you will know how.

Every person walking the earth is a slave to something or someone. The question is to whom or what? It could be your significant other, a friend, a job, a drug, a car, a house, or even your children. One of the biggest yet unknown slave masters is fear. Fear paralyzes both people and communities. People and things can control you both consciously and subconsciously. I heard the Lord very clearly express how He is grieved by the fact that so many young people are slaves to the idea that suffering in sin is acceptable or even honorable. I once had that mindset. The mindset that said being jailed was a form of credibility.

Our kids are seen as some sort of martyrs if they die in a shooting or any violent crime that results in their name on a t-shirt or Facebook campaign. Satan has our youth so brainwashed that they believe it's okay to be uneducated welfare recipients. The sad part is that the closer we get to the end of the world, the worse the epidemic gets. While the goal is educating our children and pushing them towards higher education or entrepreneurship, more and more children are being ushered into the prison system or the grave. Our children living in poor communities would rather serve two years in jail and have street cred than go to college for two years and obtain an associate degree.

The music is more intense and perverse than ever, and you can hardly rent a movie without profanity and sexual propaganda. **God wants his children back but how can you be free when you're**

unaware that you're a slave? How can you be set free when you love your master and life of bondage? People know that it's difficult to change but don't know that they are slaves. You see, we view slavery as it was depicted in the old Roots movies. But, in all actuality, the slavery we suffer today is spiritual, and it's not just black people who are chained but all races and creeds.

I once had a thought of going back into my old lifestyle of moving narcotics, getting high, and sinning on a daily basis. Then, one night, I had a dream about a slim weak man who was chained up from head to toe. He had shackles on all four limbs. I laughed inside and thought, *Why would anyone bind him with so many shackles when it only takes one to hold him down?* The Holy Spirit said to me, "That will be you if you return to that lifestyle."

This vision explains how it feels to be trapped in sin. The feelings of not being able to break loose and of constant bondage, as well as the obligation to stay in one place. A slave has no choices, and if he does, they are very few. A slave follows the instructions of his master at all times.

But the good news is that you no longer have to remain a slave. You can be free, and the keys to your freedom are in this book as well as the Holy Bible. But this not about religion or using God as some sort of last resort. God should be our first line of defense and our shield. God desires a relationship with you so that He can teach you the true meaning of living life without limitations. Life without fear is a life with God. 2 Timothy 1:7 (NKJV) reads, "For God has not given us a spirit of fear, but of power, and of love, and of a sound mind."

I challenge you to read this book with an open mind. I challenge you to see yourself within every chapter and every story. Lastly, I challenge you to use your faith like never before. Faith is simply believing in God's good will for your life in advance. Faith is having hope in God and trusting Him daily. Fear is the exact opposite of faith, so make up your mind to start casting that fear aside and living a life full of faith and trust. Believe that God only wants what is best for you as His child and believe that you are capable of breaking the chains that have you bound. It will not all happen overnight, but if you can grow in faith and understanding a little more each day, freedom will be yours in due time.

Who Is Your Master?

Is it the world's famous status quo? Status quo is simply the existing state in which things are. Maybe you have an image of being successful? You appear strong, beautiful, and well-connected. You work hard to uphold that image. Are you seeking success in an effort to keep up with your neighbors, or, even worse, your social media "friends?" Many of us are slaves to other people, and I don't mean that in a way that you are their servant. Rather, I mean you are slave to the way they see you. You are a slave to the way they think of you. We allow the people around us to hold us to a standard that is set by this world and not by God. See, God creates us all to be different and unique. The Bible says that we were fearfully and wonderfully made in the image of God. None of us are exactly alike, yet the world tells us that in order to be successful, popular, or even loved, then you have to be just like them instead of being just like you.

In no way am I making a claim that it's wrong to pursue wealth and success. God wants us to be prosperous and successful. Look at the conversation between Joshua and God. Joshua 1:8 (NKJV) states, "This book of the law shall not depart from your mouth, but you shalt meditate on it day and night, that you may observe to do according to all that is written in it. For then you will make your way prosperous and then you will have good success." This is God's desire for us all, that we would know His word and hide it in our hearts. After it is in our hearts, we are instructed to act according to the word and obey it. If you are a parent, you understand the importance of your children following your instructions so they don't get hurt or break laws. God instructs His children in the same manner. After we obey and live according to the Word, we will see success and prosperity. Truth be known, this is not the easiest route to take. Doing the right thing is hard work. Taking the easy way is tempting, especially when it benefits our wants.

Obeying God takes discipline, and we all know how much we love discipline. So, what does Satan, our adversary, do? He offers us an easier route. He says, "Hey, let's make this fast money, it's illegal but you will prosper and come up quick!" Or Satan may say, "Hey, cheat this elderly couple with a bad investment and fraudulently take their money. They don't need the money as much as you do, they're old and will die any day, just do it." Satan has so many devices for people to acquire wealth and fame because he knows the love of money is the root of ALL evil. People want to be admired and famous so much that they will do almost anything. The cost of wealth and fame is the human soul if attained by his devices.

You can live an incredible life without selling yourself. God is ready to grant you the desires of your heart, but only if it's according to His will. Some of us aren't ready to be wealthy or famous because we are self-centered, immature, or simply not wise enough yet. Wealth and fame destroy people when it is obtained outside of the will of God. How many child stars have we watched deteriorate due to drugs and alcohol? How many adult stars have we watched commit suicide, even though they appeared to be living their best lives? The list goes on and on. And it's all because Satan knows the weaknesses of man better than we do. He starts attacking our minds when we are children. He feeds our minds with his lies, media, music, and people who are willingly working for his agenda. God will never give you something that will jeopardize your wellbeing or your soul. He knows what's best for you and me before we know.

Maybe money is your master? We all need money to survive, but we must really understand our true source of income. God is our source. He gives us the gifts and talents needed to earn a living. Without Him, we are nothing. The Bible clearly states that the sun shines on the wicked as well as the righteous. There are wealthy wicked people and wealthy righteous people. The wealthy righteous understand who their source is. The Bible beautifully describes this person in Jeremiah 17:7-8 (NKJV): "Blessed be the man who trusts in the Lord. For he shall be like a tree planted by the waters. This man understands that God is the source of the rain and the seed therefore he would be a fool to take full credit for the Harvest."

Satan deceives people well—he feeds into our egos and need to be praised. For this reason, many foolish people believe they have acquired wealth or power without God's help. We all know men and women who are doing good financially and don't give God an ounce of credit. They began to make enough money to supply the lifestyle they wanted so their money becomes their god. Now they must use all their time and effort to acquire more money. I've known people who will neglect their families and work eighteen hours a day for a paycheck. I was one of them for most of my life. Some people work two or three jobs seven days a week and never make time to worship God. They never pray and never give a tithe. Money is their god, and they put all their trust in it. The only time that they consider talking to the true and living God is during times of desperation.

A basic desire of all humans is the need for appreciation or attention. Some define their self-worth by the amount of attention they receive. Men and women alike try diligently to appear beautiful and sexy. In the neighborhood I grew up in, a man's worth is measured by how many women he slept with. Therefore, the discussion about being a virgin never occurred. I was never comfortable admitting to being a virgin because I thought it was weak. To be a virgin made you look more like a punk than a normal kid in my neighborhood. This type of thinking altered my mindset and gave me the burning desire for sex at the tender age of twelve.

At twelve years old, I got wrapped up in the deceitful web of pornography, and it took me most of my life to gain freedom from it. I was never the most attractive young man, so I would hide behind my clothes and my shoes. I would do whatever it took to acquire the latest fashion. I had to look good in order to feel good. I was a slave to fashion and fitting in for many years. Like many Americans, I would spend money that I didn't have just to make sure that my children and I had some star's name brand on our clothing when, in all actuality, the only superstar that I should have been worrying about was Jesus.

Are you a people-pleaser like I was? Are you fighting hard to maintain an image that doesn't truly personify who you are? If so, it's okay because you are not alone. However, you are a slave to man and the image that the media has instructed you to uphold. If you define your self-worth and value in the houses, cars, and materials that you own, you become a slave to those materials. There's nothing wrong with having nice things, as well as nothing wrong with working hard to obtain them, but our identity should be found in Christ and not in material things that He created.

Imagine that you were an elderly man or woman on your deathbed. At this moment, you are inhaling your last breaths of life. Do you really think it would matter that you own the latest car and a million-dollar home? Do you think it would matter that you have 100,000 followers on Instagram and 5,000 friends on Facebook? Can we agree that none of this would matter during the final hour? The only thing that would matter would be whether or not God would accept your soul and allow you to enter heavens gates. During these last moments, what you contributed to your family and the world would matter more than how people perceived you or what you owned. And here's another thing to consider: God did not give you a chance to live for no reason!

You see, God expects results from my life. When you meet Him, He is either going to say, "Depart from me, you worker of iniquity" or "Come home my son, well done." I'm not afraid of very many things, but I am very afraid of meeting God without ensuring that all my work is complete. Now, it's not my works that will save me from an eternity in hell, but I long to see Him smile and say, "Well done."

I want to please God by using the gifts that He entrusted to me to help save His lost children. And while I work hard and do want to acquire nice things while I'm here on earth, I refuse to lose myself or soul in the process. I want to travel the world and shower my wife and children with as many gifts as possible, but I must understand that God is my supplier, and no matter if I'm broke or rich, He's first. HE should get the Glory and the recognition, not me. I came to a point in my life I realized that it's not about looking good in front of everybody else, and it's not about having the big title and everybody respecting me because I'm the boss. I am nothing but a servant of the Most High, God. I am a mere vessel being used by the Master Potter. I am now free of the desire to appear as something I am not, and by the end of this book, you shall be free as well.

Fear is an extremely dominant slave master on this earth. Many of us were entangled in fear as a child, and therefore we have lived with this fear long enough that it has become common. It is so common that it rules us and our behavior, and we don't even know it. Most people are afraid of dying and going to hell, so we have this theory that we can wait until we're old, then accept Jesus and live in heaven forever. The problem with that is when we wait until we are old, (1) no one knows when they're going to die, and (2) Christ came that we may have life and life more abundant. Christ didn't just come to earth so that we could all go to heaven.

There is such a thing as hell on earth. Millions are getting tormented and tortured right here on earth. So why live your entire life going through hell on earth when Christ is prepared to help you live the life of your dreams? The fear of being poor or appearing to be poor rules many people, and it ruled me for most of my life. I'll be honest and say that I wasn't as afraid of being poor as I was afraid of looking poor. You see that a lot in the African American communities. A lot of us look as though we have money, but in reality, we have no savings and no assets but lots of debt. This fear controls our financial behavior and hinders us from thinking about money from a generational standpoint. This mindset keeps us in survival mode. There's nothing wrong with being in survival mode because we all have to go through that phase at one point or another, but the person who remains in survival mode leaves nothing for their children. Many are not taught both the value of saving a mere one percent of our income and the value of interest over time.

Millions of people are slaves to the power of unforgiveness. When was the last time you held a grudge or failed to forgive someone for an offence that should have been resolved immediately rather than allowing that seed to grow? Now sometimes people hurt us in ways that we can never forget, and sometimes that pain causes us to have memories we desperately wish we could erase. In no way am I condoning the behavior that hurt you. However, I am simply stating that when you fail to forgive and release that pain to God, you end up bound by that pain. The pain, bitterness, resentment, and unforgiveness end up changing you as a person. You become negative and pessimistic. In most cases, you become harder to love.

We all know that person who is hard as a rock and overly aggressive with words. I refer to them as crabs because they are extremely hard on the outside, yet very soft and delicate under that shell. Oftentimes, this person has been abused or misused and has put up that wall of aggression as a defense mechanism. Yet on the inside, this person is full of love, sensitivity, and emotion. I know because I was that person, and some people who I love are still that person. You don't have to live behind their defense mechanisms of aggression, and you don't have to live harboring that pain in anger. Jesus came so that we could have life and life more abundant. What's more abundant than a life full of joy and peace? When you harbor unforgiveness and resentment towards another person, it's kind of like holding a glass of water—at first the weight is unnoticeable, but after a while that glass has to get put down.

Are you ready to put down that glass of unforgiveness and bitterness? You don't have to be a slave of that feeling any longer. God is holding the key, and He is waiting for you to put your hand out and receive it as a gift. You don't have to watch the person who hurt you move on with their life in anguish any longer. Right now is the time to forgive them and allow God to intervene on your behalf. After all, it has been how long since they hurt you? What have you done to fix the problem other than harbor this pain and push people away with your bitterness? Now is the time to allow God to have His perfect will in your life once and for all.

The ultimate goal of this book is to help people identify areas of their life in which they are slaves and, at the same time, set them free. As Harriet Tubman once quoted, "I could have set more free if they had known they were slaves." Right now, millions of teenagers are throwing away their lives while getting high and selling drugs. Right now, millions of men and women are harboring grief and unforgiveness while the same people who hurt them are going on with their lives as if nothing ever happened. There are millions of men and women who are using sex for both an outlet to happiness and the high that comes with sexual contact. They are putting their bodies, their minds, and most importantly their souls in jeopardy by having premarital sex with multiple partners.

Right now, there are millions of men and women who are finding satisfaction in material. Therefore, they look happy and satisfied on the outside, yet they are depressed and borderline suicidal internally. And right now, there are millions of people who are free and living their best life with the help of Jesus. Now, living for God does not mean that our lives are instantly perfect, but tailoring your life according to His word sets us free from our sins continuously as we strive for perfection. So those who were once slaves too soon can now be slaves to God and His righteousness. Being a slave to God simply means that you vow to allow Him to reign as the King on the throne of your heart. You also vow to be obedient to God and His word.

Why would I want to be obedient to God when there are so many religious people who appear to be the evilest of them all? Being obedient to God does not make you religious. If I were to give a meaning for religion, I would use the illustration of Adam and Eve in the garden. When Adam and Eve ate from the tree after they were instructed not to, they immediately felt ashamed because they knew that they were naked. So, the first act of religion was Adam and Eve sewing together some fig leaves in an effort to cover their nakedness. Religion is man's attempt to appear correct in front of God; the fig leaves were obviously insufficient, and God slaughtered an animal and covered them with the skins of the animal. And to this day, we still use cotton and animal cloths to clothe ourselves, and no one in modern society dresses in fig leaves or tree branches.

So, you have man's attempt to appear right before God—which is religion—and you have God's way, which is simply accepting His son as your savior and allowing His grace to cover all your sins. In the Old Testament, men would slaughter animals, and the blood of the animals would atone their sins, but there came a time when the blood of animals grew insufficient in the eyes of God. God knew that this time would come, so he predestined that His son would take on a human body, reside on earth for thirty-three years, and die on a raggedy cross. The blood that was shed on that cross is the blood that would cover the sins of all men until the end of time. Therefore, religion is unnecessary, and religion will not get you into heaven. Religion will not set you free of your sins or the mental issues that have you burdened and bound in slavery.

Only a true relationship with God and positioning yourself to obey Him and His word will set you free and grant you eternal life. In short, religion appears to be difficult, but God's way is really easy. You accept Him, you trust Him, and you allow Him to lead you. The Bible states in Proverbs 24:16 (NKJV) a righteous man may fall seven times, but a righteous man will also get up seven times. So, enter into the relationship with God knowing that you will fall, knowing that you will make mistakes, and knowing that you will sin. The Bible says all have sinned and fallen short of the glory of God. The Bible also says that our righteousness is like filthy rags before God. All this means is religion, as well as your attempts to be right with God and get into heaven, are all simply not enough.

We must accept the fact that we are saved by grace and grace alone. The good news is there is no class or certification needed to gain freedom from sin. You can be a man or a woman, and it doesn't matter what race you are. God's grace is sufficient to cover us all, and any man or woman that asks Jesus for His salvation shall receive it. As you continue reading this book it will help you to see the areas of your life in which you are bound and ultimately set you free as you complete the last chapter. Just keep an open mind, be honest with yourself, and know that God desires for you to be free.

Slave to Unforgiveness

Unforgiveness is an issue of the heart. If we don't take the time to cast the weight that burdens our hearts on our Lord and Savior, we will find ourselves paralyzed while the people we haven't forgiven live on. In this chapter, I'll tell a story of a young boy named Jason who was molested as a child by his uncle. At the time he was only ten years old, a baby! He couldn't fully understand if what had happened was good, bad, normal, or weird. He couldn't understand if what had happened made him gay. All he knew was that he couldn't tell his parents.

As Jason grew older, he wrestled with the memories of that night under the blanket. He struggled with how to interact with his uncle at family functions. He struggled opening up with his family and friends about his emotions. He harbored this dark secret for so long that it became normal to him to suppress his feelings. He found it hard to talk about all of his problems, as harboring his feelings had become a habit after that night. He hid one secret, which led to him concealing another. Eventually, he had a closet full of skeletons before he was old enough to understand the meaning of that phrase.

By the age of fourteen, he understood what had happened under that blanket on a deeper level. He heard stories about boys and girls who had been molested. He also heard about the consequences for the offenders. The offenders were portrayed as monsters, and in his eyes, his uncle was a monster too. This is where the seed of hatred was planted. His fourteenth year was also his freshman year in high school. So many changes were occurring at once. Hormones, high school, and puberty. This should have been one of the best years for him as far as development and exploration, but this secret created a weight around his heart. This weight hindered this young bird from getting off the ground and soaring to new heights.

Many of us are carrying around the weight of unforgiveness today, and it's hindering us from soaring to new levels in our marriages, friendships, and careers, as well as our relationship with God.

In school, Jason met a young lady by the name of Grace. They shared a total of four classes together. Grace was beautiful both inside and out. She was witty and athletic, so naturally she was a popular kid in school. During the first few months of school, he developed a crush on Grace. She knew that he liked her, and she liked him. The two grew close in school and walked home after school as well. Their bond grew stronger and stronger as time passed by. They shared their life stories during the walks home. They shared what they loved as well as what they hated. They shared their secrets. But there was one secret that Jason couldn't open up about. There was one secret that made him question his sexuality and whether or not he was a real man. This secret created a burden that in turn created limitations on what he could share with his new friend. This secret fueled an inner darkness that couldn't be perceived through his bright smile and warm eyes. He carried it around for so long that hiding it needed no effort, and even his best friend hadn't a clue that Jason was bruised and angry. Though he appeared as free as the wind, his best friend had no idea that Jason was a slave to unforgiveness.

Years passed by, and their relationship developed into love. It was their senior year, and Grace was optimistically looking at college options. Jason had no clue as to what he wanted to do after school. He loved Grace, as she was his best friend and the love of his youth. She knew him better than anyone, and he couldn't see himself without her. Grace aspired to be an attorney and, one day, a judge. She was fascinated with the judicial system and began developing a passion for helping poor citizens who couldn't afford proper representation. Jason knew nothing about what he wanted to do with his future. All that he knew was that he needed Grace in it. Jason did have a passion for children. Especially those that he knew were abused in one way or another. The incident that had happened to him gave him empathy for other children in the same boat.

Grace was accepted into a law school in Michigan. She felt the same way about Jason being a part of her future and looked for options for him at the same university. Grace knew that Jason had a passion for children and told him that he would be a great social worker. There was a nearby university that offered degrees in social work education. "I don't know, Grace," was his first response. She gave him time to think, and they prayed about it together often. Jason didn't struggle in school, but he didn't thoroughly enjoy it either. Grace on the other hand thrived in school and looked forward to furthering her education. Jason wrestled with the thought of going to college. His family wasn't prepared for him to go to college; therefore, the financial burden would rest on him alone. All that he knew was his hometown, his family, and Grace. And he loved Grace and knew that he could make a difference in the lives of others as a social worker. After months of praying and debating, Jason applied to the college that Grace suggested and was accepted. He waited until he got the acceptance letter to share the news with her.

It was the night of prom and the two shared an evening full of photos, dancing, and unforgettable memories. After prom, the two went to a favorite spot by the river to escape the crowd and noise. Jason grabbed her hand and told her that there was something he needed to tell her.

"I applied to that school and they accepted me," said Jason. Grace was so excited that she jumped in his arms and began weeping for joy.

Grace said, "I love you so much, and I was afraid that you were going to make me choose between school and you."

"Never," Jason replied. "I love you too and will follow you to the ends of the earth as long as I get to see that pretty smile every day. Plus, someone has to cook and clean up after your lazy butt." They both laughed and continued to walk by the river. The two began planning their future together that night as they walked by the river.

Fast-forward eight years. Jason and Grace were finished with school and had begun their careers as an attorney and social worker. The pressures of life began to weigh on Jason. He had student loans and bills due. On top of the financial pressures, Grace was pressuring him to get married. *Get married?* He thought, *I'm not ready to get married.* But he loved her with all his heart, and he knew that he didn't want to lose her to someone else. So, he purchased the wedding ring and proposed. She, of course, accepted and the two joined as one. Everything seemed perfect on the outside, but on the inside, Jason was struggling. Grace would often argue that Jason seemed distant at times and that he wouldn't open up enough about his feelings. However, Jason believed that harboring his feelings was part of being a man.

"Men don't complain or talk about how they feel, they just suck it up and move forward," he would often say.

The lack of communication and openness put an immediate stress on the relationship. After a few months in, Grace reached out to a marriage counselor within the church that the two attended. She pitched the idea of marriage counseling to Jason, and he vehemently rejected that request.

"I don't need anyone trying to get into my head," he yelled. "We don't need anyone trying to tell us how to live. We are perfectly fine."

Jason insisted. He made so many excuses as to why they didn't need counseling. Grace gave up on her first attempt for them to see a counselor, but now she was forced to carry the weight of Jason as well. The weight he was carrying from an incident that happened nearly twenty years ago was now affecting his wife.

Grace dealt with the issues of her marriage as well as she could. She was raised in the church and had developed a relationship with God at an early age. She prayed for Jason and their marriage constantly. Yet she was often tempted at work. In the beginning, she could handle it with ease, but as time progressed and Jason failed to change or even attempt to change, she found herself desiring more. There were dozens of attractive men in her world. Men that seemed to have their emotions in check and their priorities in order. So, she decided to tell Jason that if he didn't change his ways that she would find someone different.

"I love you and only you, but I can't live like this," cried Grace. Jason hated the thought of Grace with another man. The threat of losing her was enough to push Jason into the counselor's office.

The first few sessions were easy for Jason. Questions were directed at both sides, and the counselor focused on a few of Grace's weaknesses at first. Grace was a bit controlling, and her life as a new attorney caused her to neglect her husband more than she realized. Jason felt relieved and thought, *See, she's crazy, I ain't crazy. There's nothing wrong with me.* But as they got into the fourth session on the topic of transparency and opening up about everything, things changed.

The counselor asked the question of whether Jason felt as though he could share anything and everything with his wife. One tear fell from his left eye. He couldn't reply. He didn't want to lie. But he couldn't release that secret. The counselor asked if they could pray together and end the session on that note. The counselor prayed, "Heavenly Father, I ask that You give us the ability to see that Your strength is made perfect in our weakness. I ask that we lean on Your understanding and not ours. Please give Brother Jason the ability to know and understand that there is nothing that he could say or anything that he has done that wouldn't be covered by Your mercy and grace. Give him the strength, God, to open up and release the pain that is burdening him."

Jason opened his heart as the counselor prayed. He received the prayer in his heart and in his spirit. Jason began to cry.

Jason wept for minutes as Grace just rubbed his back and wiped his face. "I'm not gay," were Jason's first words! "I'm not gay, and I didn't want that."

"What are you talking about?" asked Grace.

"When I was ten years old, my uncle touched me and made me touch him," replied Jason. His face was filled with shame. "I didn't know what was happening until I got older, but I didn't want that. I have never told anyone. I couldn't tell anyone. I know I should have told you, baby, but I couldn't. I didn't know if you would think I was less than a man or if you would judge me. So, I bottled it up. I got used to bottling my emotions. I thought that was the right thing to do."

Grace wrapped her arms around Jason, and they wept together. The counselor sat in his chair in shock and said, "I think we should end here and give everyone time to collect our thoughts and pick back up next week."

During the ride home, Jason realized how free he felt. That weight was lifted off his heart.

"Grace, I'm so sorry for my behavior," he said. "I didn't know that one little secret was affecting you so much. I'm sorry for not being completely honest with you. I'm sorry for pushing you away."

She accepted his apology, and that moment caused their bond to become stronger than ever. Jason spent the rest of the week telling Grace about all of his fears and concerns. They talked about his hatred towards his uncle and every other child molester walking the streets. Every time that Jason opened up about his feelings, Grace grew closer and closer to him. They were becoming best friends again. Their flame was reignited, and the passion that fueled their love ever since they were teenagers was alive again.

Jason learned a powerful lesson about how releasing the secrets of our past pains sets us free from a bondage that not only affects us, but also the ones we love. However, there was still a problem. He still harbored hatred for his uncle. He couldn't allow the hatred for his uncle to reside in his heart and potentially harm Grace someday. It was as though he loved her more than himself, and her wellbeing was more of a priority than his own. One night, Jason prayed. It was around

4:00 a.m., and it was quiet throughout the entire neighborhood. He paced through his house and whispered to God, "God, how can I free myself from this pain that has afflicted me for almost twenty years? How can I be free from this burden and move forward by Your grace? So many days I have thought of killing him and killing any man that would molest a child. But your Word says, 'thou shall not kill,' so I know that's not right in your eyes. How can I be free, oh Lord?"

After he finished speaking, he knelt and heard a quiet, still voice say, "Forgive him as I have forgiven you, go home and forgive him. Then you shall be free."

Jason went back to bed confused and questioning what he heard. Forgive him? That can't be God! What happened to an eye for an eye? *Why can't he feel the pain that I've been feeling all these years? Why can't I knock him out cold first?* Angry thoughts of rage and punishment consumed his mind for the rest of the night. All of which were contrary to the command of God. The enemy always speaks in contrary to the commands of God. When he woke up, he immediately told Grace what he had heard after he had prayed. Grace knew the Word and immediately knew that it was indeed the Spirit of the Lord speaking to her husband. Therefore, she didn't say a word other than, "Let's obey." It was a Saturday morning. The two had breakfast, got dressed and began the five-hour drive back to their hometown.

They arrived back in their hometown early that afternoon. Before going to his uncle's house, Jason stopped at the river they had walked next to after the prom. "Let's pray," he said. So, the two walked next to the river and held hands as they prayed. Memories began to surface as the two walked down memory lane. Suddenly Jason's heart was filled with great joy and strength. As he looked back over the times that Grace and he shared, he couldn't help but realize how blessed he was. He had the love of his life by his side. He had a great career as a social worker and helped lots of people overcome some of the same issues that once hurt him.

Even though he had been abused as a child, he overcame it and used that experience as a fuel for his motivation to help others. God kept Jason and used what the enemy had meant for evil for Jason's good. He thought about the dozens of children's lives that he had impacted and suddenly realized that he was a strong man. In the same place that he realized how much he loved Grace and couldn't be without her was the same place that he realized how God loved him the very same way.

As he stood on his uncle's porch and rang the doorbell, he rubbed his hands together nervously. So, Grace grabbed his left hand and squeezed. He instantly relaxed, but his heart was still pounding through his shirt. His mouth was dry, and, for a second, he thought about turning around and going home, but the door opened. It was his auntie.

"Hey baby," she yelled in excitement. "What a pleasant surprise."

She grabbed the two and pulled them inside. She asked, "What brings you back home? We normally only see you two during the holidays."

"We were in town and dropped by to see Uncle, if that's okay," Jason replied.

"Of course that's okay, but I have to warn you that he isn't in the best shape these days," she replied.

"What do you mean?" Jason asked.

"Your uncle had a stroke a few years back, and he's been in a wheelchair ever since. He can barely speak," she added.

He headed down the hallway to his uncle's room and saw the old man bed-stricken and grey. His uncle looked up at his face, and Jason saw fear in his eyes. The two stared at each other for a few moments before Jason approached the bed. Grace approached the other side of the bed, leaned in, and kissed the old man on the forehead. She then said to Auntie, "Why don't you show me some pictures of Jason when he was a kid?"

"We always argue that his head has doubled in size over the past twenty years," she said jokingly. The two burst out in laughter as they left the room. Jason and his uncle never lost eye contact. Jason took another step and grabbed his uncle's hand. He then whispered, "I forgive you, Uncle, and I love you."

Tears beginning to roll down his cheeks, Jason said it again, "I love you, and I forgive you. For years I hated you and wanted you to die, but I was wrong. I forgive you."

His uncle struggled to move, but he reached out slowly and grabbed Jason's hand. He then whispered, "Jason, I'm so sorry."

He went on to say, "My father used to do to me what I did to you. I'm not making excuses, but I was a very damaged and evil man. When I had this stroke, I had no choice but to reflect on my past. I hurt you and many others. I asked the Lord to come into my heart and forgive me of my sins, but I couldn't have peace and rest until I knew that you forgave me too."

He then said, "You were a bright young man full of life and purpose. You didn't deserve to be handled like that and I'm sorry. I hate what I did, and I'm so sorry Jason. I love you, and I'm so proud of the man that you have become. God has truly favored you. You have a beautiful wife, great job, and you escaped this small town for bigger and better things. You done good, son."

That day, Jason left the burden of unforgiveness at the bedside of his uncle. He even felt a little love and sympathy for the old man. He prayed with his uncle and told him he loved him one last time. Grace and Jason hugged his auntie and headed home. As they drove home, Jason began to cry.

"Why are you crying?" Grace asked.

Jason replied, "I just feel so bad for him. He can barely move or speak. His life is basically over unless God performs some miracle. And while he is here bed stricken, I'm at home thinking about punching his lights out all these years. But if I had known what I know now, I would have forgiven him years ago. I carried all that hatred and anger for a man that endured the same thing I did. Only difference is that I didn't repeat the cycle but instead found a way to break it in my life and the lives of others."

Grace grabbed his hand as he drove and replied, "God's timing is perfect. All that matters is that you made it through. You can't beat yourself up. You survived. Now leave all that mess here and let's move on into our beautiful, bright, child-filled future."

Jason choked and said, "How is two kids a child-filled future?"

Grace replied while she laughed, "Well I was thinking four."

The two went back and forth about the number of kids they would have for the rest of ride.

That next week at work, Jason could feel a huge difference within. He was more focused. He was a better communicator at work and at home. Telling his wife about his day was easy. Grace loved the enhanced communication, and Jason loved the attention that he was receiving in return. The flame was reignited. The following Saturday, Jason received a call from his Auntie.

"Jason," she cried. "Your uncle died in his sleep last night. He has gone home to see the Lord, and I'm just so happy that he got to see you and Grace before he died."

Jason's heart dropped, and the only words that he could say were, "I'm so sorry, Auntie."

"Don't be sorry baby," she replied. "He gave his heart to the Lord four years ago after years and years of running. He's with the Father now. No more pain, no more being stuck in that bed, and hey, I can live now. God knows what He's doing at all times."

"Yes, Auntie," Jason replied. He then hung the phone up and cried softly.

Death is guaranteed, yet another day of life is not. If the shackles of unforgiveness or secrets are holding you back from being free, seek God for the key. God doesn't want us to be slaves of unforgiveness and secrets. He wants you to be free to live. He wants you to let go of the past and embrace the future. Seek God in a quiet place. Lay your heart and pain at His feet. When you're done, just listen for His instructions. When you receive the instructions, obey them. No matter how much they may contradict your own logic and reasoning, just obey Him. Your freedom depends on your ability to seek God's instructions and, more importantly, to obey them.

Slave to Money

In 1 Timothy 6:10 (NKJV), it states, "for the love of money is a root of all kinds of evil." As I said before, money is needed to survive in the world in which we live. The Bible also teaches us that money answers all things; however, the desire and lust for money is what breaks our relationship with God. Money is the god of many people, and God clearly instructed us to place no other gods before Him. God designed us to depend on Him, therefore the lust for money always drives us to depend on ourselves and our own abilities rather than relying on the Father.

In my younger years, I was infatuated with hip hop music. The music would teach us that if you have money to burn and all the latest trends, then you're on top. The music taught me that selling drugs for a fast buck was a way of life. In no way am I bashing hip hop. Hip hop raised me, and there a lot of good artists out there with a positive message. On the other hand, there are a lot of misleading artists who will later regret the way they lead so many to Hell. As parents and leaders, we must guard what we allow our children to pour into their spirits by way of music. Take the time to analyze some the lyrics from your child's favorite artists.

Money, power, and respect where at the forefront of hip hop's message when I was a teenager. These were all the things that I didn't have at the tender age of fourteen, but I developed a lust for them, and my actions changed. I smoked my first blunt at the age of fourteen. My taste for music developed at fourteen. My friends were all smoking weed and listening to hard core rap music, so this was the norm in my neighborhood. I was headed nowhere fast, but at fourteen, I thought that I knew everything. My father was absent, and my mom and stepdad couldn't tell me anything. In my mind, I was grown.

Hebrews 13:5 (NKJV) says, "let your conduct be without covetousness, be content with such things as you have. For He

Himself has said, 'I will never leave thee nor forsake thee.'" As a child, I grew up in what some would consider a project. Lower income housing, majority black and Puerto Rican population. I remember looking across the street and wishing that I lived in a nice home at Bicentennial Village. I even wished I was white or at least biracial at times. It seemed like they had it way better than we had it. The school buses didn't even come to our neighborhood. I remember when I lied about where I lived and told schoolmates that I did live in Bicentennial. I was coveting my neighbor's home before I could even define coveting.

This is a trick of the devil. He magnifies our current situation. He deceives us into believing that our neighbor has a life that we need. Some kids, teens, and even adults are coveting their neighbor's house. Men want to be women, blacks want to be white, poor want to be rich, and vice versa. Very few are content, and many don't believe that God is with them and won't forsake them. So, we look to status, which in most cases come from money and fame. Where do we go when we feel forsaken or out of place? What does a child do when media and music define the requirements of being beautiful and successful? They define beauty as perfection covered in makeup. They also define success by how many followers you have and how much money you make.

This next story is about me. I'll start at age fifteen. At fifteen, I was a decent athlete. I started on the football and basketball teams. I was a decent student when I was focused or wasn't high off marijuana. I could have easily put forth more effort and gone to college and played ball. I played power forward and tight end. I was a natural born leader with a gift in writing. I was always a leader in the crowds that I associated with. I had many talents, but all I wanted to be was a drug dealer. I wanted to make fast money and have street credibility.

My mother didn't believe in buying us name brand shoes and clothes. In both elementary and middle school, I remember getting clowned for the way I dressed. I needed glasses since age six, so that made matters worse. Now it was my time to shine. I remember skipping school with my best friend and hanging out in the hallways while selling weed and crack. I remember the conviction and guilt I felt when some of my friend's parents came and bought from me. I even sold to some of my family members. I felt convicted about it, but it didn't stop me. I was a slave to the money and would do anything to keep it coming.

I would rob, sell crack, weed, PCP, whatever I could get my hands on. Yet all I was doing was buying clothes and shoes, jewelry, and rental cars. I remember my uncle telling me that if all I was going to do was buy shoes and clothes, that I might as well get a job. So, I got a job, but I still sold drugs because I was greedy and grown. No one could tell me anything.

When I was sixteen, I dropped out of school and sold drugs full time. By this time, I was selling more than the year before but had nothing to show for it other than a decent wardrobe. I remember standing in that hallway waiting for someone to come and buy. I could clearly see that I had been standing in the same spot for a year. I wasted one year of my life and couldn't get a second back. But I didn't stop, I was bound. So, I set my mind to go harder in the streets. I was living with my stepdad at the time. I remember him being mad at me for flunking off the basketball team. He was angry and told me that I was a just a screw up. Those words hurt me deeply, and even though I knew he was right, I couldn't take it. I packed a bag and left in the morning and never stayed with either of my parents again.

I was sixteen and living with a girl in her twenties. She knew I was underage and didn't care. She was attracted to me because her child's father, who had died earlier, looked like me. I was attracted to her slightly but really just needed a place to stay. It was a toxic situation that didn't last long. I remember my mother coming over and instead of leaving with her, I would jump out the window and run away. After

I broke up with the young lady, I stayed with friends for as long as I could. I stayed with crack addicts. I slept in cars and hallways.

All I could think about was making money and appearing to be on top of my game. In the streets, I was respected. My neighborhood loved me. At the high school, I was feared after hurting another kid and breaking his jaw. I felt like I was so cool at the time, but I was a complete fool. I was running the streets with a pocket full of money, but I was homeless and losing time. I was so worried about street status that I didn't even consider the fact that my mother was not sleeping because she was unaware of where I was.

When I was seventeen, I got involved with a young lady who was seven years older than me. I was living with my aunt at the time. We would hang out in secret. But what's done in the dark always comes to light. She ended up getting pregnant, and we had a little girl when I was eighteen. That beautiful baby girl was just what I needed. She motivated me to do more than just think about myself. But I was still motivated in the wrong ways. I was still selling marijuana. I had sense enough to stop selling crack as the jail sentence was much longer for a crack conviction, but I started buying and selling weed by the pound. Business was so good that I needed two cell phones. My daughter had an abundance of clothes and lots of toys. In my mind, I was a man and a great provider. But I was still a fool. Everything that I had given her was from evil deeds and drug money. My princess deserved so much better than that.

One Friday night, it was my turn to keep the baby, and I needed to reup and buy more drugs. I left the house with $8,000 and a small amount bagged up in case I got a call on the way. The guy I was riding with was being followed, and neither of us knew it until we were pulled over by the police. I ended up in jail that night. I had just lost $8,000, my car was being impounded, and the police wanted me to tell on my friend. With all these conflicts surrounding me, the only thing I could think about was how I left my baby girl.

Reality hit me at that moment. I couldn't raise a child from jail. My father was never there for me, and on the day she was born, I bent my knee and vowed to God to be better than he was. I made bail that Monday morning and sold everything I had. I sold the drugs I had left. I sold my scales and my gun. I switched my phone number and moved on from the drug game. I couldn't bear the thought of missing my daughter's life, so I was done for good. This was my first drug charge as an adult. Though I had a large amount of cash and weed bagged for sale, God gave me favor, and I only received a misdemeanor possession charge.

I started working in a chicken plant at age nineteen. My grandmother worked in the plants for twenty-five years, and she talked me into going down there to apply. I hated the thought of working in a stinking chicken plant, but I would do anything to make sure my daughter had what she needed. God gave me favor in the plant, and I worked my butt off. At the time, I was going to Dr. Norman Hutchins' church. One Sunday he taught about how we as people worship money over God and how, until we put God first, we could never be blessed. He taught about the curses that come with worshipping money. He taught about how, when we gain money doing evil, nothing good could ever come forth.

"A good harvest is produced by a good seed," he said. His words were punching me right between the eyes because of all the evil I had done in my life. But one thing really inspired me in his message. He taught me about a sacrificial thousand-dollar seed. He talked about how he struggled to give that much the first time. But when he decided to sow that amount into the Kingdom of God, it changed everything. His career took off, and his money problems went away.

I had to try this for myself. Everything that I had done in the past wasn't working. I wanted to show God that I no longer worshipped money. I wanted to show God that I could be a blessing to His kingdom, for He had always blessed me. So that February, I took

$1,000 from my income tax refund and gave it to the ministry. Less than one month later, I was promoted to supervisor at the chicken plant. My salary increased from approximately $19,000 to $33,000 a year. I was in awe. My thoughts were, *God is real, God is amazing, His word is true and alive, it works.*

This wasn't the only time that I have sown a $1,000 seed and reaped a harvest quickly. Once I was connected to a ministry with a powerful pastor named Apostle Norman. I loved her and wanted to bless her for the church anniversary. But I was really struggling financially. The heating bill at my old home was killing me as this was during the recession of 2008. Heating oil was four bucks a gallon, and we needed to burn 500 gallons a month to keep everyone comfortable. By faith I put $1,000 dollars in an envelope and before I could even give it to her, I was called into the complex manager's office. I had only been with this company for a couple of months, but they loved my work (it was really God's favor on my life). He praised me for my results and promoted me. That day I received a $15,000 raise and my bonus potential went from ten percent to twenty-five percent. I hadn't even given the seed, and God blessed me. I gave the seed that Sunday, and my testimony blessed the church.

When I worshipped money and did evil to obtain it, I had nothing to show for my efforts at the end of the day. I lost years chasing what I saw on TV and heard on the radio. I have friends who are still doing time in jail. Some of my friends and family lost their lives for that fast money. The love of money is the root of all evil. But when I learned to exalt God over money, God blessed me in ways that I never could have done alone. With God first, I didn't have to worry about going to jail or getting robbed or killed. When I was not humble and thought I was the man on the street, God humbled me in that cage. When I humbled myself, God lifted me in the workplace.

Thank God that I was no longer a slave to fast money and status! But was I still a slave to money? Did I trust God or money? For years,

I truly believed that I was free from being a slave to money, but I was wrong. I say that I was wrong because when I made the decision to quit my job and start my own business there came a time that I simply did not have enough money to make everything work. I would pray and ask God for financial relief, but my doubts were much stronger than my faith. When I had thousands of dollars in the bank and all of my bills were paid, I had a certain level of comfort and trust in that position. However, when the money was low, fear ruled my emotions.

My level of trust in the God that I claimed I served was nowhere near as high as it was when my bank account was full of cash. Money was my master And I didn't know it until I frankly ran out of money. God wanted me to meditate on His law day and night, just as he had Joshua to focus on His law. However, my focus was on earning more money. Instead of focusing on God's law and trusting that he would supply all of my needs while I completed my first book, I instead stressed and searched the internets for jobs which were all a waste of time.

I didn't talk to my wife about this fear until it became unbearable. This fear was controlling my mood and choking my communication with her; therefore, it created a strain on our relationship. My wife knew that I was hiding something, and in my mind, I wasn't hiding anything wrong like cheating or drugs. Yet I was hiding the fact that I was afraid, and I was hiding the fact that my pride was completely shattered. I was accustomed to being the breadwinner and a pretty good supplier for my family. Now I was in a position where the only thing I could do was trust God. God would then lead me and my wife as he led Jesus into the wilderness. Our wilderness journey started the week after we got married.

My wife and I got married in Delaware, and the Monday after we returned to Iowa, the owners of the company that she worked for reported to everyone that the company was shutting down. Nine months prior, my wife and I purchased a $180,000 home, and we both had other debts to satisfy as well. We had recently started our company FireStarters, but we were nowhere near being profitable. My first instinct was to live by faith! *Walk by faith, Allandis,* is what I told myself. I would encourage my wife that everything was going to be okay and that God would provide as he always had, but I still had this fear. Fear of losing our home and fear of failing as a man and husband.

All of this fear only resided in my heart because I was not in complete control of the money situation. I did not have a six-figure salary to depend on anymore. But I had something far greater, I had a God who would never leave me or forsake me. I had a God that would supply all of my needs according to His riches and glory in Christ Jesus. The plant ended up shutting down. I got a job making fourteen dollars an hour. My wife tried a few jobs but none of which paid as well as what she had before. My wife and I once had a combined income of just under $200,000 dollars per year. We were now making a combined $30 per hour, yet our bank accounts did not dwindle, and we lost absolutely nothing. God blessed us during this season of lack, and my wife was an absolute genius with our finances.

My wife and I went through a period in our life in which we were in the wilderness. We set aside our sins and dedicated our lives to God, and God walked with us as we were tested financially as well as emotionally. There were times in which I wanted to give up. There were definitely times that I thought about reverting back to some of my old ways. But I knew the end result, and I knew that I couldn't be the best husband, father, or leader without keeping God first and staying consistent.

One day my wife and I sat down and looked at our finances. My wife pointed out the fact that we were making roughly forty percent of what we once did, but we still had enough money to pay all of our bills and chip away at our debt. I remember stressing about finding a publisher for my first book, so my wife and I prayed one day. I remember crying out to God and telling Him that even if I never published a single book, and that even if I had to paint RV's for the rest of my life to pay my bills, I still trusted Him, I still loved Him, and I would still live for Him. That moment changed everything. I had a sincere heart, and I went to God honest, humble, and broken. Approximately two weeks later, I received a contract from a publisher who believed in my book and wanted to put it into print.

Another area in which I struggled was within our business. I simply told God that I didn't know exactly what I was doing in our business. With a sincere heart I asked Him to connect us with the right people so that we could be more effective in our business. Soon after I made this request to God, He connected me with a young man who was having great success in the area that I was lacking but was failing in the area that I was succeeding. A partnership with this young man didn't form, but he gave me the clues I needed to gain our first major contract with the largest protein manufacturer in the world.

On the contrary, if I had strictly trusted in my own ability to acquire money or certain achievements, I don't believe that these results would have been attained so quickly. I probably wouldn't have achieved them at all without God's help. When I finally realized that I was still a slave to money and that my trust in God was nowhere near where it needed to be, I decided to push my fears to the side and to finally put my trust in God.

The Bible says that money answers all things, therefore money is not a bad thing and money is not evil. The lust for money is the root of all evil but having money and using it to take care of your family is not evil. Having money and using it to bless the kingdom of God is not evil. Trusting in money and holding it to a higher esteem then you hold God is where people go wrong. It's where I went wrong. Thank God that He took me to a place in which I could no longer depend on money, and I can no longer just trust in only my abilities. God took me to a place that made me realize that I don't really know anything. God took me to a place and made me realize that I'm not that talented nor that smart. Once I admitted to God that I didn't know everything and that I really needed His help, God moved.

The Bible says that God exalts the humble and that God also humbles those who exalt themselves. I have been on both ends of that proverb. I have been exalted when I was humble as well as humbled when I was full of pride. I came to a place in which I was completely broken. I had almost given up all hope that my dreams of being an author would come to pass. I had submitted my manuscript to countless publishers and sent out queries to dozens of agents only to be shot down and denied. But as soon as I put my trust and my faith in God and God alone, an editor on Wall Street in New York sat down at a meeting and truly saw value in the writings of my first book. God granted me favor again. God's favor is greater than anything we can do on our own. I pray that you get to experience God's favor for yourself immediately.

I admonish you to not make the same mistake that I made and wait until you are financially strapped to trust God. Trust God now with your finances. The number one way of proving to God that you trust Him with your finances is to give ten percent of all your income to a solid spirit-filled church that not only preaches the gospel but lives the gospel. Malachi 3 (NKJV) instructs us to give ten percent to God's store house so that there would be supplies and food in His house. If you give ten percent consistently, it's just like sowing a seed into good ground. The Bible clearly states that you will reap what you sow.

Giving ten percent will be a test because as you write that check or as you prepare to put that money into that envelope or offering plate, your mind will begin to think of the ways that you could be using that money rather than just giving it away. Therefore, it's a test--who do you trust? Do you trust God and His word, or do you trust money? We've all been faced with this test, and if you fail on the first attempt don't worry because you're not the first, and you won't be the last, but don't give up. If you can give 10% to an effective spirit field ministry, I guarantee you will see the fruits in your own life in due time. My wife and I began tithing, and we truly believe that our giving, as well as our trust in God, is truly what kept us from losing everything during our wilderness journey.

If God would do it for us, He'll do it for you too. For God is not a respecter of person. God loves us all the same regardless of sex, race, or creed. Trust in the Lord your God with all your heart. It is God who gives you the ability to make the money. God gave you that skill and that ability. God is keeping you in good health so that you can perform your job or run that business effectively. So, take a second to really think about what it would be like if God were to simply cut you off in this moment. It happens to people every day. Sometimes it's a divorce. Sometimes it's an illness. Sometimes it's a drug addiction. Sometimes it's strictly emotional. Many different circumstances can cause us to lose balance without having God on our side to see us through. God has carried you this far, but for some reason you may have thought that you did it all on your own. If you think you did this all on your own, you're wrong. I don't want you to hit a brick wall before you can look up to God and say, "Thank you, and I trust you." If you no longer want to be a slave to money, simply repeat this prayer. God, I trust You and only You. You are my provider and the reason I live. I will never again exalt money or material higher than You. You are my king, and I love You more than things of this world. If you can say this prayer with a pure heart and clean hands, then I believe that God has set you free from bondage.

Slave to Sex

Sexuality had been a part of Aaron's life for as long as he could remember. It all started on the playground. The older girls would rub their body on his, and he enjoyed it, so he didn't stop it. This behavior sparked a curiosity that grew into a flame that later consumed his body. Aaron was eleven years old the first time this happened. He was also eleven years old the first time that he saw pornography. Aaron's older cousin always allowed him to watch TV at his house, and for some reason one day, he hit the play button on the VCR. What he saw on that TV amazed him and infatuated him at the same time. He didn't tell anyone about it, but he snuck over to his cousin's place and watched that tape whenever he could. He had a new best friend. He thought about it all the time. His body started reacting to it in ways that he didn't understand.

Aaron was now twelve and had no clue what he was into. But he did know that it was wrong, and that he couldn't tell anyone. His cousin was not spending much time away from home, and Aaron wasn't getting time to watch the porn anymore, so he stole the tape and took it home with him. Anytime that his mom was gone, Aaron was watching it. When she went to work or to the store, he was watching it. He had a routine where he would turn the TV volume all the way down and listen for her coming up the steps of the apartment. When he heard her coming, Aaron would stop the tape and switch to cartoons. He did this for months.

Aaron was a slave to that tape, and his young soul didn't even know it. He thought about it all the time and watched it every chance he got. One day, Aaron's mom's boyfriend found the tape and asked him why he had it. Aaron was extremely embarrassed and unsure of how to explain it. Aaron just shut down and bottled everything up. He couldn't talk about it, and soon, his mother's boyfriend left him alone. He didn't really care about Aaron, and his mom didn't know how to talk to him about sex, so he was off the hook. Yet the sin wouldn't leave him alone.

Aaron soon found other ways to get his fix. Showtime and Cinemax after dark. Pay Per View channels were sometimes slightly visible so little Aaron would sit there and stare at the blurred lines, looking for a woman's image. At his family's homes he would find porn magazines and cards with naked women on them. Aaron would hide them and hold onto them like they had great value. These images had a hold on his young flesh and were affecting his spirit. The images that he was embedding into his mind were soon transferred to the women in his life. Aaron started seeing friends and even teachers with lustful eyes. Sex was on his fragile mind most of the time, but he had a good way of hiding it. He was always shy and preferred being quiet because it kept him under the radar. But on the inside, his heart was screaming for help. Aaron wanted to do what was on those tapes. He wanted to be with a woman so that he could feel what he had fantasized about on many occasions.

Aaron was fourteen years old when he lost his virginity. There was a young girl in his neighborhood who had a crush on him. He didn't care about her, but he wanted that feeling. He wanted badly to feel what he witnessed on that tape. He had to have that feeling. The two were playing on the playground at night when she kissed him. Their hands grabbed each-other's private areas and Aaron's heart started racing. She asked if he was afraid, and of course he said no. But in all honesty, Aaron was terrified. This was his first time, but it wasn't hers. She helped him, and before he knew it, it was over. He walked her home and barely said a word. All he could think about was that feeling and how he wanted more of it. The biggest mistake Aaron made was that he failed to use protection. Thank God for his mercy because Aaron could have easily gotten her pregnant or received an STD that day, but that wasn't the case.

They continued their relationship for the rest of the summer.

They would meet up wherever we could, just to have sex. There were no feelings involved, it was only a sexual encounter. When Aaron looks back, he's amazed as he was only fourteen and she was only thirteen, yet they were what the world calls, "friends with benefits." After their relationship ended, Aaron just moved on to the next girl. Aaron always had someone on standby to fulfill his need. He was an addict and slave to the lust of his flesh. He went to church all the time, but Aaron had no capacity for God because his juvenile heart was filled with so much lust. Aaron recalls lusting after girls in the church and thinking impure thoughts while in the house of God. Sex was always on his mind.

Aaron remained a slave to sex well into his adult years. He had done things that he was truly ashamed of, and he made mistakes that could not be undone. But through it all God has shown Aaron grace, and he has loved him in spite of his past disgusting ways. One day, God gave Aaron the perfect gift in a spouse. Everything that he ever wanted and needed was in her. But he knew that in order to keep her and love her the way she deserved to be loved that he needed to grow up. So, Aaron bowed down before God and asked Him to grant him the strength to set aside his childish ways and to please mold him into the man who He had called him to be. Aaron prayed constantly for God to continue to mold him and make him the best husband he could be. God did just that.

Aaron made a conscious decision to set aside his foolish ways because he knew in his heart what he found in his wife was something that he could possibly never find again. True love is rare, and to be equally yoked is a privilege that not everyone gets to experience. Aaron's wife taught him so much about being selfless, and she has taught him how to examine himself from a perspective other than his own. When we commit fornication or adultery not only do we sin against God, but we sin against our own bodies. When will you start to cherish the body that you've been given and treat it as the temple that it was designed to be? You can be free from the slavery of sexual sin, but you must want to be free. This freedom cannot simply be for God, but it must also be for you. You must know that you deserve to be free, and that it is God's will that you be free and pure. The desire has to come from your heart. If you desire freedom and believe that God is able, I guarantee He is willing if you would just ask and believe that He is able.

Next, I'll tell a story about a young woman who was once a slave to sexual sin, but you would never know it. We will call this young woman Sarah. Sarah was a well-known CPA in her town, and Sarah was loved and admired by all who know her. Sarah was married with two children, and to the public's eye, Sarah lived the perfect life. Sarah and her husband had been together since junior high school, and they got married two months after graduation. Sarah was pregnant with their first born at the wedding, and it was this pregnancy that brought the pressure of marriage from both Sarah's parents as well as her husband's. Sarah's husband was thrilled to get married, but Sarah got married full of doubt, insecurity, and regret.

The first five years of the marriage were a bit rocky for the couple. They battled with their youth, financial struggles, and insecurities on both ends. Stress began to enter the marriage and eventually pushed the two apart. Not only did stress create a division in the marriage, but physical appearance had changed; therefore, Sarah did not find herself attracted to her husband the way she once did. As a young woman, Sarah had needs but she loved her family, and she did not want to be the reason for separation or divorce. She suppressed her needs and tried her best to hide her unhappiness in plain sight.

The office that Sarah worked for was expanding, and they brought in a new CPA by the name of Blake. Blake was an attractive man and very charming. Sarah was put in charge of training Blake; the two spent quite a bit of time together. Blake was also married, and one day over lunch the two shared their stories. Blake and Sarah were amazed at how similar their stories were. They were both married at a young age, they both had children, and they both had arrived at a place where they had fallen out of love. At this moment, the two were not attracted to each other when a friendship developed. Blake and Sarah worked together very well, as they were both efficient and very passionate about being the best CPAs within the company.

A few months after Blake started with the company, they decided to open another office, and they named Blake the head of that office. Blake and Sarah had grown used to seeing each other and working together, therefore they remained in contact constantly through text message. One day Blake sent a message to Sarah stating that he missed her, and that text message changed everything. Sarah replied that she missed him also and wished that she could see him. Blake invited her to lunch, and there it began. It seemed as though the two hadn't seen each other in months, but it had only been a few days. After lunch Blake walked Sarah to her car and hugged her, and after the hug, they shared a kiss. Embarrassed and full of shame, they both hurried to their cars and just sat there in shock.

What have I done? Sarah thought, *I am not a cheater or an adulterous, what was I thinking?* Blake texted her and immediately apologized.

"I'm so sorry Sarah," he wrote.

"I didn't mean to disrespect you," he added. "I just really missed you and somehow, I got carried away in the moment. Please forgive me."

"Don't be sorry" Sarah replied. "To be honest I enjoyed it. Can we meet after work tonight and just talk you and I?"

"Of course," Blake replied. So, after work, the two met, talked, and held hands the entire time. There was a connection there that neither of them could resist. Surely enough, after they got together, the two began kissing again—this time passionately and shamelessly. That moment led to the two being alone in a hotel room. They were both extremely nervous about the act that they were about to commit and the possibility of being caught. They proceeded and made love.

Sarah and Blake went home to face their families pretending as though it were another normal day. On the inside, they couldn't stop thinking about what just happened. Sarah had suppressed her physical needs for so long that this moment only fueled her desire for more. This sexual encounter was what her marriage was missing. Her marriage was lacking passion and romance. Her body felt like a woman again, and her passion was reignited. The one time with Blake turned into two or three times a week. Being with him was all that she could think about, and she spent her days daydreaming about what they shared. Sarah knew that it was wrong and knew that if anyone ever found out it could hurt her family, but she couldn't stop. Sarah was addicted to that feeling. Sarah had become a slave to the lust of her flesh.

The little desire that Sarah had for her husband had now diminished completely. Her body and mind only longed for Blake. Her husband knew that something was wrong, but he held on to Sarah as though his life depended on it. He was afraid of losing her. He did his best to make the marriage work and remained focused on the children and their needs. Sarah, on the other hand, was spiraling out of control. She was spending hundreds of dollars on hotel rooms and buying Blake gifts. The secret affair was weighing on Sarah. She had no one to talk to about the affair, and that weight began to weigh on her heart. That weight turned into shame and guilt and eventually led her down the path of depression. Sarah had no clue how she ended up being depressed yet still addicted to the affair that her and Blake shared. How could her body be temporarily satisfied yet her mind permanently subdued?

"Am I in love, or is this just lust?" Sarah asked herself. "Do I leave my husband for a married man or do I continue with this love affair until I eventually get caught? I love my husband and what we have, and I am ashamed because I never really gave him a chance to fix our issues. I don't love Blake as he is selfish and childish, but I love the way he makes my body feel. But I can't live with the shame anymore.

I can't bear the thought of my children ever finding out what I've done." And in that moment, Sarah locked the doors of her office and got down on her knees behind her desk and cried out to God. She asked Him for forgiveness and mercy. She also asked Him to direct her on how to resolve this issue. God led her to repent and be honest.

That night Sarah knelt before her husband and confessed her sins. She told him that she had not been attracted to him and somehow, someway, had fallen out of love with him. She explained that even though she was not attempting to have an affair that it still happened. She said that she was ashamed, and that she totally understood if he wanted a divorce, which she wouldn't fight. Her husband replied that he needed to make a confession as well. He confessed to a porn addiction and stated that since the two were not having sex that he was watching porn daily and satisfying his need in that manner. He also told his wife that he wasn't as attracted to her as he once was, as pornography has caused her not to shine as she once did in his eyes. Finally, he confessed that he was ashamed and felt in his heart that he was a failure. He took responsibility as the leader of the family.

"So, what do we do now?" asked Sarah.

Her husband replied, "Do you still love me?"

Sara answered, "Yes, but do you still love me?"

Her husband then said, "Yes, I love you, and we can get through this but only on one condition."

"And what's that?" replied Sarah.

Her husband answered, "We must somehow get God's help."

He went on to say, "We need God's help, and we need God's guidance in order to overcome this moment. Without God's help, my jealousy will only drive me to find out who your lover was and take his life. I know that's not the answer but the more I think about it, the more I want to kill that man. I need God to take that anger from me and to heal our marriage." Sarah wept in shame

Her husband went on to say that he had been listening to a

preacher online, and he felt like the preacher was talking to him. He felt like God was calling him to serve Him. Sarah then told her husband that she felt the need to pray in her office that day even though she hadn't prayed or even thought about God since her mother used to make her go to church when she was a child. Her husband then said, "The preacher always says that God would never leave us nor forsake us."

Sarah and her husband held hands for the first time in over a year and prayed in their living room. They asked God to intervene and help save their marriage. They also asked God to free them from the temptation to fulfill the lusts of their flesh. Once they finished praying the two made a promise to each other to bury the past and move forward into the future. They also promised each other to openly communicate about their feelings whether good or bad. They both made a conscious decision to put God first.

Sarah's husband introduced her to some of the online sermons that he was listening to, and the two developed a deep desire to learn about God. Soon after, the two found a good church and began attending faithfully. One Sunday, the pastor preached a sermon about letting go of shame and guilt, and he told a beautiful story about how God casts our sin into a sea of forgetfulness never to be mentioned again. The pastor then instructed everyone who was battling with sin or guilt to come and lay that sin at the altar and never mention it again. Sarah and her husband both walked to the altar and dropped their sins. Immediately, a weight was lifted from both of them, and that weight was replaced with a smile. That very moment Sarah and her husband were not only freed from sexual sin, but they were also free from the guilt that tormented them since they had decided to walk away from its captivity. No matter what we get trapped in, God always has a way of escape.

Freedom from sexual sin is not easy, but with God's help, it's not difficult either. God wants you to be free, but how bad do you want it? Are you willing to confess your sins to God and to ask Him to free you according to His will? Can you change people, places, and things? If you can do these few things, you can be free immediately. Warning! Shame and guilt will attempt to torment you. When this happens, lean on God and His word. For His word reminds us that when we accept Christ, we are new creatures, and the old you is dead. Trust those words as truth and speak them over your life constantly.

Slave to Fear

Fear paralyzes people and controls our minds. It hinders our imagination and stalls our creative processes. Fear is one of the greatest slave masters used by the enemy, and no one can deny its effectiveness. Fear and love are two of the greatest forces on Earth. For the longest time, I was afraid that I would never find a woman whom I truly loved. When I did find her, I feared that I didn't deserve her and would lose her. Fear of loss racked my brain until I began creating scenarios that didn't really exist.

I became paranoid and started to worry about things that were not even a problem yet. At the same time, my wife-to-be was going through the exact same battles. In this chapter, I'm going to breakdown five different types of fears that we all battle with. We will talk about the fear of being poor. We will talk about the fear of being accepted or rejected. We will also talk about fear of physical and mental illness. Lastly, we will also talk about the fear of success and failure.

Fear of Being Poor

The fear of being poor affects us all. In Matthew 6:25 (NKJV), Jesus expressed how humans shouldn't be worried about what they're going to eat or how they're going to pay their bills because our Father in heaven cares for us and shall always provide. Jesus gave a description of how the birds don't work yet they always eat and how the lilies of the field are more beautiful than Solomon's wardrobe, yet they don't sow eat either. Our Father, who takes care of the birds and lilies of the field, cares for us as much if not more. Therefore, we shouldn't worry. However, the enemy is always sowing seeds of doubt into our minds. Satan is working around the clock with millions of spirits or fallen angels constantly planting fears into our minds. These fears are introduced to us by the news, social media, and through word of mouth. So, on one hand you have God saying, "Don't worry, I have everything covered." On the other hand, you have Satan saying, "You're not going to make it, you're going to be poor, and you and your family are going to starve." The devil is a liar, and the truth is not in him.

I remember growing up and always wanting to appear to be wealthy. In actuality, I always had what I needed, but as an immature and selfish young man, I could only focus on what I wanted. Therefore, I followed the instructions of the enemy and sold drugs in my own community to get name brand shoes, designer clothes, jewelry, and any kind of drugs that I wanted. If I had listened to God during these years, I could have been content with what I had. I could have worked a job for the things that I wanted, and I never would have torn down the community that raised me.

But the enemy has a way of coercing us into doing things that not only serve our own selfish purposes, but also damages the environment in which we live. The fear of looking poor really drove me as an adolescent. That fear drove me to do things that were immoral and that could have caused me to do a lot of time in prison if I had been caught. However, God's grace was sufficient for me, and His mercy covered me before I even knew what His mercy and grace were. God's mercy and grace are covering you right now as you read this book. God is saying, "Trust Me and follow Me." God is saying, "Believe in Me and know that I have your best interest at hand." But many of us are stuck listening to the voice of our adversary, who is controlling you through anxiety and fear. Your anxiety and fear are driving you to do things that are not beneficial to either you or the people you love.

As an adult, I was often controlled by the fear of my children growing up in poverty. Therefore, I would work countless hours on the job to stay ahead. I would often miss out on the time that I should have spent with them just to make sure they had more than enough.

My fear of being poor, or even appearing to look poor, mixed with my ambition and drove me to work sixty to seventy-hour weeks. My children would only see me on the weekends. Yet much of that time during the weekend I spent resting so that I could be effective at work. So, if time is the most valuable asset that we all have, why did I give so much to my profession and so little to my children? Because I was afraid of being poor, and I was really afraid of my children growing up the way that I did. More importantly, I didn't trust God. I trusted myself, and I trusted my own ability to provide. So, at the end of the day my faith was in me, not in God, and I handled things all wrong. From the outside, I looked like a hard-working father and a provider, but on the inside, I was afraid and stressed. I sacrificed all my time to ensure that my family had what I thought they needed when, in actuality, what they needed most was my time and attention. Fear drove me to do things that hurt myself and the people I loved.

So, we can't allow our fears and anxieties to steer the ship of our lives. We must instead do the right thing, which is to allow our Lord Jesus Christ to be the captain and guide our footsteps. If we do the opposite and create our own paths, then the end of that path is always destruction. My destruction—and the results of creating my own path—was that my children don't have many memories of me being there for them. When the divorce was final, my children made it very plain that all I ever did was work, and that I didn't spend enough time with them. It would be easy for me to say, "Hey, I was doing what I had to do and that I was a good provider."

The truth of the matter is my fear caused me to fail in certain areas as a father. Looking back, my children always had more than enough, and God always blessed the works of my hands. Looking at the lives of some of my peers, I could tell they didn't make as much money as I made, but they still have their children. And more importantly, their children still want them to be a part of their lives. There is no greater story that I can tell than of my own failure—how I allowed my fear to control me as an adolescent and as an adult. Don't be like me, for your sake be better than me! Please, be better than me!

So, what is the opposite of being afraid of poverty? The opposite of being afraid of poverty is trusting in God that He will supply all of your needs according to His riches and glory. In order to trust God, we must have faith, for without faith it is impossible to please God. How do we have faith in something or someone that we cannot see? That is the true test! This can only be accomplished by first accepting Jesus as your Lord and Savior, and then developing a relationship with Him through prayer and reading His Word. The more you read His Word, the more evidence you will find of Him continuously supplying for His people through means of miracles and other people. The simple recipe is to pray, believe that He hears you, and read His word so that it can transform your mind. It has worked for me and countless other people. Therefore, I guarantee it can work for you.

Fear of Acceptance and Rejection:

In this section, I am going to tell two stories. The first story is about a young man who is afraid of being accepted for who he is, and the second story is about a young lady who is afraid of being rejected for who she is. We'll start with Antoine. Antoine was a young African American male who is growing up in a city of approximately 30,000 people. He was raised by his mother and grandmother. Antoine was the oldest of four children, and Antoine loved his family. Antoine was an intelligent young man, a gifted writer, and everyone loved Antoine. He had a personality that was magnetic, and when he spoke, people listened. Antoine lived in a lower income housing community. There were two gangs, and drugs were common in Antoine's community. Antoine was an honor roll student, and Antoine was listed among the gifted writers at his school.

Antoine's mother worked two jobs in an effort to pay all the bills, as well as buy groceries and clothing. Therefore, after school,

Antoine hung out with a few of his friends in the neighborhood. Antoine was a freshman in high school, and some of the kids that he hung out with didn't go to school. They sold drugs all day and made rap music about the lifestyle that they lived, and this negative environment was a strong influence on Antoine. Antoine's friends were extremely proud of the money they made. They made money the fast and easy way, and they boasted about the fact that they have no accountability along with the best clothes and jewelry.

Now on the other hand, Antoine was proud of the fact that he was an honor roll student. He was also proud of the fact that he loved to write and speak in front of crowds. But he had no one to talk to about these achievements. He was afraid that his friends wouldn't accept him for the intelligent and gifted young man that he was, so he would limit himself in their presence and use the slang that they used while pretending to have no real interest in school at all. Antoine was strongly influenced by his friends due to their material gains, therefore he stooped to their level in an effort to be accepted. Antoine was afraid of attempting to be accepted for who he truly was.

Many of us can relate to Antoine. There are some people who we can be ourselves around, and there are others who require us to stoop to their level in an effort to be accepted. Antoine truly had the power and the ability to influence his friends in a positive way, but his fear ruled him. Therefore, he didn't attempt to influence his friends. One day after school, Antoine approached his friends as they are smoking marijuana. Now Antoine had no interest in smoking marijuana at all until he saw how his friends were laughing and joking relentlessly. In the eyes of Antoine, they were having a great time. Antoine's friends offered for him to take a hit of the drug, and Antoine said yes. Antoine began to feel carefree and somewhat drowsy. Suddenly everything that his friends said was hilarious, and Antoine was having a great time under the influence of marijuana. Luckily, when Antoine went home that night his mother wasn't home from work yet, and no one knew that Antoine has taken his first hit of marijuana.

All of a sudden, Antoine started hearing about being high in lots of different songs, and Antoine started seeing people getting high on TV often. These visual displays created a desire for Antoine to get high again. Antoine went back to his friends and smoked marijuana for the second time. This time Antoine enjoyed it even more than the first. Soon Antoine began to smoke marijuana every day after school. Smoking marijuana made Antoine very relaxed, and eventually it diminished all of Antoine's motivation towards school. At first it was just missing homework assignments.

After Antoine got high, he never cared about completing homework assignments, and, in turn, his grades began to drop. In school, Antoine's mind began to drift, and getting high seemed to be Antoine's number one concern. The child who was once proud of the fact that he was gifted and thriving in school was now simply drifting through his days. Marijuana has a way of simply stealing all motivation and desire to improve. So, after about three months of smoking marijuana on a daily basis, Antoine had devolved into a D student.

Antoine's motivation to be a writer or a speaker was quickly replaced with the desire to make fast money and write rap music about the lifestyle that Antoine witnessed in his own neighborhood. Now Antoine had not lived this lifestyle, but he was ashamed of who he really was while being infatuated with what he really wasn't. Therefore, he clung to the lifestyle of his friends and pushed aside the gifts that God had given him. Antoine's mother received his report card and was shocked that her oldest son, who was always so bright and well behaved in school, was now on the verge of failing. Antoine began to display an "I don't care" attitude, and his responses to his failure were so vague that his mother had no idea what had happened to her son and how she could help him. As a mother who feared God, the only thing that she knew to do was to cry out and ask God for answers. I believe that it is the prayers of Antoine's mother that kept him out of jail and eventually led him back to the right path.

Antoine ended up failing two classes that year and found himself in summer school. But in summer school, Antoine met one of the greatest teachers he could have ever come across. His name was Mr. Martin. Now Mr. Martin was an African American male, and Mr. Martin was extremely educated. But what Antoine respected the most about Mr. Martin was that he was extremely disciplined, and he seemed to be proud of who he was. Mr. Martin was very tough on his students during summer school. This discipline that Mr. Martin placed on his children was exactly what Antoine needed. Antoine ended up passing Mr. Martin's class with an A+. Antoine's mother began attending a new church, and the pastor there was a gifted man. This pastor was a recording artist and a writer. Yet what impressed Antoine most about this pastor was the fact that he was young and proud to be who he was.

One Sunday the pastor preached a sermon about fear. And Antoine held on to the scripture in Psalm 23:4 (ESV): "even though I walk through the valley of the shadow of death, I will fear no evil for You are with me." Antoine saw his neighborhood as the valley of death, plagued with drug addicts and marijuana smoke. The ground was littered with empty drug baggies, and no matter what time of day you could hear sinful, hateful music playing loudly. Antoine believed that the Lord was with him after this sermon. No matter where he was, the Lord was with him, and he didn't have to fear anymore.

That day, Antoine asked the Lord to remove the fear from his heart and to make him proud like Mr. Martin and his pastor were. This childlike faith moved God, and on that day, He granted Antoine's request. The next Monday after school, Antoine went out to speak to his friends. They offered to pass the marijuana to Antoine, and he pushed it away. Antoine proudly told his friends that God had better plans for him than to waste precious time sitting around smoking weed as life passed them by. Antoine was afraid and thought that his friends would clown him or talk down to him for taking a stand and not smoking. However, the opposite happened, and they praised him and told him that they wanted to be more like him. One of his friends said that they always saw something special in Antoine, and that if he ever saw him wasting his life again that he would beat him down jokingly.

During his sophomore year, Antoine began to excel in school like never before. God completely removed all fear from Antoine's mind. Suddenly, Antoine was as bold as a lion. Antoine knew that God was with him no matter where he went, and that confidence gave Antoine the ability not only to succeed in school but also to motivate two of his friends in his neighborhood. Two chose to enlist in job core and obtain their high school diplomas. By making the decision to no longer fear being exactly who he was, Antoine turned himself into an influence rather than remain the scared little kid who had been influenced by the evil which surrounded him.

Are you afraid of stepping out and being exactly who you are? Are you prepared to completely hand that fear over to your Lord and Savior and began walking in the strength that He gave you on the day that you were born again? Think of the strength that Christ needed to boldly walk this earth, knowing that He was the son of God, yet He didn't even profess that He was the Son of God. The Bible says that He thought it was not robbery and didn't boast about being a Son of God; instead, He was a mere carpenter. The Bible refers to Him as a servant. You are a son of God the day you accept Christ as your savior. Therefore, walk in humility and boldness, being proud of who you are, as you are.

I love the story of Jesus in the Luke 4:16 (ESV), "When his time came, Christ entered the synagogue and began to speak and read the scriptures aloud." Christ was entering his ministry by influencing those who would in the near future follow Him. Maybe there are people that God has assigned to your life to follow you. As long as you walk in fear of who you are, those followers won't know who you are, and your influence is going to waste. Don't allow yourself to die without fully utilizing the influence that God has blessed you with. Be confident in the person you were created to be. You are a child of the Living God—you are a servant, a leader, and a powerful person. Open God's Word and find out just how powerful you are.

In this next story, we will dig into the life of a young woman by the name of Jane. Jane was a single mother of a beautiful three-year-old son. Jane and her son's father were no longer together, and Jane was beginning to suffer from depression due to being alone.

Jane and her son's father were high school sweethearts, and Jane became pregnant during her senior year. The relationship between Jane and her son's father did not last due to their youth and their having separate goals in life. After a couple years of fighting and slowly growing apart, the father walked out.

Jane never really saw herself as beautiful, and for some reason she felt as though her son's father was too good for her. In the back of her mind, she had always felt as though there would come a day that he would reject her after finding out who she truly was. Jane spent all of her young adult life controlled by this fear until, one day, it became a reality. Jane's family had never been religious, and Jane had never considered the fact that God was real. One day, one of Jane's coworkers dropped her an invitation for a church revival that was taking place the following month. Jane thought that the invitation was silly, but for some reason she took it home and slipped it under a magnet on the refrigerator.

Jane's relationship with her son was strong and beautiful. That little boy was the center of her world, and everything that she loved was in him. The fact that he looked so much like his father would hurt Jane at times and even cause her to miss him. By no means was Jane an unattractive woman, but in Jane's eyes she was horrible and unworthy of having anything good. It was unclear to me where this feeling of lowliness originated. Jane's mother and father both loved her dearly. Jane was shown both love and affection as a child. She was the youngest of three, but her older sisters were often praised for their beauty, and Jane was often praised for her gifts. Jane was often referred to as the smart one, and though she was just as beautiful as her older sisters, Jane only clung to the words that she was the smart one.

Jane began trying to get back into the dating world, so she used social media to her advantage. All of her pictures were of herself dolled up with makeup and eyelashes while appearing to be living her best life. The fake smiles and the cropped images were highly effective, and Jane collected thousands of likes. Social media gave Jane a sense of acceptance in the digital world but the fear of being rejected paralyzed Jane's mind in reality. There was a young man who had a crush on Jane. His name was Jake, and he always commented on Jane's pictures. Jake was a couple years younger than Jane, but he was extremely outgoing and very active within his church community. One day Jake mustered up the courage to ask Jane out for dinner. Jane refused to go out to dinner with Jake but still communicated with him through social media. Jake didn't give up after his first attempt, and the two ended up meeting after work one Monday to take a walk near the river.

The two instantly became friends as Jake worked to earn Jane's trust. Jane had a tremendous wall up, and even though she thought that she was hiding her fear flawlessly, Jake picked up on her insecurities the first day. Jane couldn't hold eye contact for more than a few seconds. Jane had on way too much makeup, and she was a bit overdressed for a simple walk. However, Jake did not say a word about these insecurities. Jake instead commented on how beautiful she was and how perfect she was in his eyes. These compliments were well received by Jane, and she began to let her guards down. After two or three meetings at the river, Jake finally got that dinner that he wanted. The two had dinner at a quiet restaurant, and Jake spent the whole night listening to Jane's story about her high school sweetheart and of her walking in the shadow of her two older sisters. Jake knew that Jane was beautiful and intelligent, but at that moment he was unsure of how to get Jane to see herself the way that he saw her.

Now Jake was a young man, but he was raised in the church. He knew the Bible very well, despite his youth. A particular scripture came to his mind. Ephesians 2:10 (ESV) says, "For we are His workmanship, created in Christ Jesus for good works."

Jake said to her, "God created you perfect, and if I could change one thing about you, it would be nothing."

One tear fell down the right cheek of Jane, and in that moment her love for Jake began to flourish. They spent the rest of their night laughing and joking as they slowly got to know each other.

Jake walked Jane home, and as her mother left from babysitting Jane's child, the little boy ran out shook Jake's hand. This made Jane very nervous, as her son had only ever known his father. Jane was also afraid that her son would make Jake run, just as his father ran. But it actually did the opposite. Jake saw that little boy full of love and life and only wanted to get to know him more. Before Jake left, he asked Jane if she would be his guest at his church's revival service this coming Saturday and to bring her son. She told him that she had never gone to church and really had no interest, but for his sake she would consider and let him know as soon as possible.

Jane and her son went back into the house, and her son went to the refrigerator for some milk. He couldn't reach, so he called his mother for assistance, and as she grabbed the door the invitation that she received earlier that month fell to the ground. Suddenly Jane noticed that the invitation was for the same revival that Jake had just invited her to. Was it a coincidence that Jane was invited to the same event twice by two different people? Or was it a sign from God that this is where she needed to be this weekend (God oftentimes sends confirmation)? Jane texted Jake and told him that she would accept the invitation to go to the revival. However, she was uncomfortable and would likely only stay for a little while. That night Jane did something that she had never done in her life. After her son fell asleep, she prayed. She asked God that if He was real, could He please give her sign of what He wanted from her that weekend at the revival?

Jane went to the revival with Jacob on that Saturday afternoon, and there was a young woman ministering to a crowd of hundreds. Jane was nervous, as well as full of doubt and fear. She had never been to anything like this; therefore, she was completely out of her comfort zone. Suddenly the young woman minister began to testify, and her testimony grabbed the attention of Jane. The young lady began to explain how she went through high school depressed and never saw herself as beautiful. She explained how she got wrapped up in drugs, alcohol, sexual relationships, and even criminal activity.

"All of these sins and negative behaviors were fueled by my fear of being rejected by people who I thought were friends," she said.

The woman continued, "One day I found myself all alone in a psychiatric ward."

She explained that she had taken so many drugs that she overdosed, and the people she had thought were her friends had left her to die in a hotel all alone. She had been found by the cleaning lady the next morning and rushed to a nearby hospital. Due to her age and the number of drugs found in her system after she had been released to the hospital, she had been admitted into a psychiatric ward for thirty days. And during these thirty days, none of her so-called friends had come to visit her. The only person who had come to visit her had been her mother. Her mother had been full of faith and had believed God for many things. The most important thing that her mother had believed God for was that he would set her daughter free from the slavery of drug addiction, depression, and negative influences.

The young minister vividly described a feeling of being trapped at war within herself. She also talked about the feeling of being bound by countless chains. The only person that would visit this young minister in a psych ward had been her mother, and one day out of desperation, the minister had asked her mother to pray with her. The mother had prayed with her and had cried the entire time, but during this prayer had been the very moment that the young minister had been led to Christ. She wept as she explained how, from that moment, her chains began to fall off her. She began to see herself as the person she truly was. After being released from drug abuse, she found out that she was beautiful, both inside and out. She discovered that she was full of personality and talent.

At the end of her speech the young minister invited anyone from the crowd to come forward and pray that same prayer that she had prayed with her mother on the day that she had been set free. Jane felt a tugging at her heart and began to cry. Jake immediately grabbed her hand and led her to the altar. Jake stood behind her as the young minister began to pray for Jane, and on that day, Jane accepted Christ as her Lord and Savior. Instantly, Jane felt a sense of relief and a difference in her heart that simply couldn't be explained by words alone. For the first time in her life, she knew that God was real, and she felt it by the evidence of His love.

It took some time as Jane developed her relationship with God to find out for herself how beautiful and amazing she truly was. God began to show her that not only was she intelligent, but she was loved and a great mother. As Jane matured in her faith, her light began to shine brighter than ever. Her sisters and her mother noticed the change. Her colleagues at work noticed the change. But Jake noticed the change more than anyone. The love between Jake and Jane only grew stronger as time progressed. The two not only had a relationship with each other but watching each other grow in Christ motivated them both to pursue God even more. So young Jane went from walking in the fear of being rejected to walking in the complete knowledge of who she was.

Who was Jane? Jane was just like all the young women out there who are caught up in the standard set by a world full of fakes. A standard that says, "You must be this weight and your hair must be this long and you must wear these clothes this way." But that's a lie. God created us all different! God created us all unique! But God created us in His image, so even though we are different we are all beautiful in our own ways. As soon as Jane accepted Christ and began to study His word for herself, she became enlightened as she learned God's plan for her life.

If you are a slave to the fear of being rejected, I want you to simply ask God to set you free. The only rule is that when you ask Him, you must believe that He will do it and prepare yourself to be free. There may be things about you that you can improve like your weight or maybe you're a smoker. God can help you make those adjustments, but it does not mean that you're not beautiful exactly as you are. Cast down those thoughts of ugliness and cast down those thoughts of worthiness. You are worthy to be loved, and you are worthy to be appreciated.

The Fear of Death and Illness

This next story is about a husband and wife who co-pastor a church in a small city. We will call the husband Paul and his wife Portia. Paul and Portia were the co-pastors of a vibrant congregation. Paul was a business manager for a Fortune 500 company, and he was working his way up to become a partner. Portia was a cosmetologist with a thriving beauty shop ten minutes from their home. Portia had been struggling with an anxiety disorder for most of her life. She feared not being in complete control over several areas of her life (I believe that anxiety is simply fear mixed with lack of control). For a while, Portia had the ability to manage her anxiety disorder until, one day, Paul came home with the news of being diagnosed with pancreatic cancer.

Now one of the things that Paul and Portia were very proud of was their faith. Paul and Portia had been in the ministry for many years and had lead hundreds of people to Christ. They two had witnessed many miracles together. But there was another level of faith needed when it came to believing that God would move on their behalf! Suddenly Paul and Portia were overtaken with the fear of Paul dying and forgot about the fact that God was able to do anything. The very first morning after Paul was diagnosed with cancer was the absolute worst. Portia had been in great control of her anxiety disorder for as long as she could remember, but suddenly, she dropped her guard. It was as though she had never had control in the first place.

She lay in bed crying out to God, asking Him how her and her husband could be so faithful to Him and how they could serve so many, but yet this could still happen to them? Paul, during his prayer to God after receiving the diagnosis, asked the same questions. But something in Paul would not allow him to cry nor show weakness. Paul knew that he was the head of his household. He knew that he had a responsibility to lead his church. Therefore, even though he was afraid, he decided to set his fear to the side and carry on with his mission. The problem with trying to suppress fear is that everything that is within us eventually surfaces. As humans we can hide and try to camouflage for as long as possible, but eventually the truth must come to light.

Portia was the number one organizer at the church, and her entire business ran off her command. She also kept her house in pristine condition while scheduling all her children's activities, meals, and family functions. Suddenly, Portia was under a severe anxiety attack and controlling her anxiety was near impossible. She felt like she had control of nothing and therefore lost control of everything. She was terrified that without her husband, she would lose control of everything in her life. She was terrified that if she lost her love and her best friend, that everyone else would leave her as well.

The fears that Portia was fighting with were all false. Most of the things that we worry about or fear will never really happen, but the adversary makes us believe they will. The adversary was using Portia's fears to paralyze her during a time that her family and friends needed her faith and mobility more than ever. You see, Portia was who many would consider to be a prayer warrior. She has led women's groups in prayer. She has helped pray many women through the exact same circumstances she was faced with right then. But for some reason, she did not have enough faith to pray for herself. Many of us have been the same way. We believed that God could work miracles out for everyone else, but when it came down to our situation, sometimes we just didn't have the faith to believe that God would do it for us. I'm telling you the reason for that was fear. Sometimes people didn't know that fear was controlling them. Sometimes people didn't know how to ask for help while facing what they feared. Therefore, we were forced to wrestle with that fear alone.

Meanwhile, Paul was doing everything in his power to be the rock for his family. He went to work every day and continued leading his ministry as though nothing had changed. He loved his wife and his children on another level because he was afraid that he would die soon. In secret, he went and met with his attorney to prepare his will. He verified that all of his life insurance policies were in order, and he ensured that his wife's name was attached to all of his assets. His fear had him preparing for his death. There was nothing wrong with being prepared for death, but God wanted Paul to live. God wanted Paul to subdue his fear and to place all of his faith and trust in Christ. God also wanted Portia to subdue her fear of being controlled by an anxiety disorder and get back on track with leading her family.

One day, an elderly woman stopped by the church after service and asked Paul and Portia for a moment of their time. Paul and Portia invited the woman into their office, and they all sat down over coffee and began to talk. The woman proceeded to tell Paul and Portia that the Lord had sent her there to tell them a story. She went on to say that the story was about a wise man with the heart of David and that his wife had the wisdom and beauty of Naomi. These two had been together for many years. God had kept a hedge around them the entire time. The two possessed an extraordinary faith, and because of their beauty, wisdom, and pure hearts, people were attracted to them in large numbers.

These two possessed that mustard seed sized faith, and sure enough they had witnessed mountains be removed in other people's lives. But for some reason, they had no faith whenever it pertained to the mountains within their own lives. Lots of people walk the earth with multiple shackles attached to them. But this couple had only one shackle each. The man was a slave to the fear of death, and the woman was a slave to the fear of mental illness.

One day, the Lord looked down from heaven and decided that the time had come for Him to personally deliver the keys to His children and remove the shackles. So, He sent an old lady who had overcome cancer twice. And this same old lady who had survived cancer twice had also conquered bipolar disorder and severe depression. The same old lady attempted to take her life after her husband died out of fear of being alone. But this old lady was blessed enough to meet an angel. That angel reminded her of the many times that God had delivered her and told her that God had need of her to share her testimony to help his children overcome.

"So, I stand before you today as a witness that you are free, and that you have no need to fear death or any type of mental illness," she said. "Now I don't know if either of you have cancer And I don't know if either of you are battling with a mental illness, but those tears that are falling from your face are telling me that you have need of what I'm telling you."

Paul and Portia wept as they held each other's hands tighter than ever. Neither of them had words to say other than, "Thank you, Jesus."

The old woman concluded her story with the fact that the Bible says that there's power in the name of Jesus. She told them whenever their minds started to entertain the fear of death or mental illness, all they needed to do was call on Jesus and believe without a shadow of a doubt that He was right there. Paul suddenly felt a weight removed from him, and from that moment on he knew that he would live. In his heart, he knew that he had always been strong enough for this moment and that he would overcome this moment. In his heart, Paul always knew that he would be faced with something huge like this. He believed that he was prepared to face his giant. Paul looked at Portia and spoke over her life. He told her that she was the best wife he could ever ask for, and that if it was not for her, him and his children would not be as blessed as they were then. He told her that there was no need to be afraid of him dying because he wasn't going anywhere anytime soon. Finally, he reminded her that she was in complete control over her mind and her emotions.

Paul and Portia prayed in the presence of the woman, and when they opened their eyes, the woman was gone. They did not hear a door open or hear any footsteps leaving the room. She simply vanished. Paul and Portia knew without a shadow of a doubt that this woman delivered a message from God. This message gave Paul the strength to face his battle with cancer head on. For the Bible says that man shall not live on bread alone but off every word that comes from the mouth of God. And sometimes God uses people to deliver His word. Portia still had some doubts left in her heart, but God would use Paul to guide Portia through this next season of trial. Paul left his fear at the feet of Jesus and walked forward in full faith that God would deliver him from his illness.

Portia began to trust God and her husband like never before, and she too was delivered from being controlled by anxiety. That next Sunday, the two stood before their congregation and delivered the news that Paul was battling cancer. Paul proudly and boldly proclaimed that he would live and not die. The two never spoke of the old woman that came to visit them until after Paul successfully beat pancreatic cancer. Portia and Paul never saw that woman again. God's message, which was delivered through the elderly woman, was the key to unlocking the shackles of fear that bound the two. There is freedom in God's word. You can always find the keys if you seek His Face.

Fear of Failure

During this last story, I will use myself as the character as I speak to my own fear of failure. As a child, I saw my biological father twice. When I turned thirteen, for some reason I hoped that he would call me on my birthday. He didn't call. I made up my mind that I would never hope in anyone because I feared being let down. Being let down hurts a child, and the scar remains today. I made my mind up that I would never be like him. In my eyes, he was a failure. Later in life, I had children of my own, and I even helped raise four children who were not mine. My number one goal was to be a great provider and to make sure that I gave them the type of love and support that my father never gave me. My dad really wasn't a good example of what to be, but he was a great example of what not to be. I'm not blaming my dad; I love him, and I have forgiven him for everything, but this is still my truth. I hope this story doesn't hurt my father or any other father who failed to raise their kids properly. Just know that God can fix anything.

When I was twenty-two years old, my ex-wife and I had a set of beautiful twins. On May 26, one died. At the time, I was serving God, and I was a youth teacher at our church. After my daughter died, I got so angry with God that I turned my back on Him. I ran from God and back to the same sin that bound me prior to him setting me free. I went back to drinking and smoking. All this happened during the height of the recession, and I felt as though I would never make enough money to get ahead and be financially prepared in the event of another devastating life event. When my daughter died, I didn't have life insurance for her, and I didn't have the money to properly hold a funeral for her. All of that gave me a sense of failure as a father. During this time, my family and I were living on the East Coast. I decided to move everyone down to the state of Georgia. The company that I was working for opened the plant down there, and the cost of living was much cheaper, so we packed up and moved south.

My family and I lived in Georgia for approximately three years, and towards the end of our third year, things got rough at work. I did not agree with the way the company was being ran, and I was afraid that I would fail along with the management. I was successful in my role, and I helped the team prosper in many ways, but there was one thing happening there that I couldn't stomach. So, I didn't pray and ask God for guidance—instead, I started looking for another job and jumped at the first opportunity I saw. My family and I found ourselves in South Carolina in a very odd place. Needless to say, this opportunity did not work out for us, so I had to humble myself and crawl back to Delaware. The company that I previously worked for allowed me to take a lesser role.

I worked there for approximately one year before I took a role with another great company thirty miles away. Well this company was phenomenal! They had great people, and I was making more money than I ever made in my life. I was one of the best managers they had on the team, and our directors had high hopes for me and my future with the company. I had high hopes of being a plant manager by a certain age. This company paid well and had a great atmosphere, so people never left. My fear of failing to reach plant manager status by a certain age caused me to take another position for a promotion with a company in Pennsylvania. Recently, at my current company, I was passed up for this position. It wasn't because I wasn't qualified or even because I wasn't the best person for the job--I was simply the least senior. A peer who had been there eight years longer than me received the promotion. It was fair, but I was selfish and ambitious, so I moved on.

I started my new position in Pennsylvania, and it wasn't long before I realized that this was the worst decision of my career. Everything that I was used to such as structure, goals, accountability, vision, teamwork, and morale simply didn't exist there. I was in hell, or so it seemed. I worked sixteen-hour days, six days a week. I was miserable. So, I began looking for another job after working there for approximately one year, but I couldn't move. I was there for three years, and I just couldn't move. Finally, after three years, I was free, and I found myself working for a great company down in North Carolina.

After five months of working in North Carolina, I was recruited by a complex manager whom I had met in Pennsylvania. He was a great leader, and I had grown to respect and admire him. I took a chance and followed him all the way to Iowa. In Iowa, I went through a lot. I grew to the level of plant manager and beat my goal by seven years. I was an instrumental leader of a startup operation. I went through a divorce. I found the perfect woman and my future wife after the divorce. I also battled with depression and the fear of failing as a plant manager. Let's not forget the fear of failing and losing this perfect woman whom I adored.

So, what did I do when all of these fears controlled my mind? I ran. I ran to China. I ran to Mississippi, only to find that I couldn't be without her. Every move that I made over the last fifteen years led me to her. My fears tried hard to control me and drive me away from Iowa, but in Iowa, God had a gift for me. This gift was my wife, my best friend, my business partner, and my everything. My fear almost paralyzed me and caused me to lose what I had been looking for my whole life. We all say we're looking for true love and someone who understands us. Someone beautiful and perfect in many ways. I found it, and for the first couple of years I was controlled by the fear of losing it. I was a slave to the fear. I was afraid that I wasn't enough for her and that I would lose her.

Fear told me that I would be better off leaving her and getting another job far away where no one knew me rather than stay and lose her. So, I had a choice to make, and that choice was to return to God and finish what we had started many years ago. That choice was to trust God even though He sometimes led me into the wilderness to be tested and tried. I am no longer a slave to the fear of failing as a husband or failing as a leader. I have learned that my failures are lessons and temporary defeats. I have also learned that each and every one of my failures had a seed for my success.

If I run because of failure or if I stop the process, I will never see the end result. How many times have you stopped a process because of a minor setback or a stumbling block? I chose not to run this time, and I chose not to remain a slave of my own fears. As a result, I am free. The fruits of my freedom are that my wife and I run our own debt free company called FireStarters. I no longer have to work long dreadful hours for a company that dictates my salary and schedule. I have completed one book. This book is my second book. I married my best friend. I live a life full of joy and prosperity. All because I cast my fear to the side and decided to trust God with everything in me. We all fear failure, but a wise man once told me that failure is not an option. You will have temporary defeats and you will have minor setbacks. It is your responsibility to capture the lessons of those temporary defeats and keep pressing forward. Press forward with faith in God. Press forward with faith in yourself. Press forward with tenacity, courage, and love.

Repeat these words: I am no longer a slave of fear. Those chains have been broken, and I am free in Jesus' name. For whoever the Son sets free is free indeed.

Slave to Man: The People Pleaser

Let's just be honest: we're all people pleasers in one way or another. We all long for the feeling of being accepted. We all love the feeling of being popular and liked among our friends and family. To an extent, there's nothing wrong with making others happy and being accepted for who you are within your community. However, the keywords are "for who you are." If God created you perfectly, and if you are the apple of His eye, then what right do you have to live your life pretending to be something or someone that you're not? If you are living your whole life struggling to please others by wearing a mask instead of living your life in a fashion that pleases God, you are a slave to man. You are a slave to a culture that doesn't care about you.

I want you to take a moment and think about anyone that you struggle to please. I want you to consider the amount of effort that you consciously and subconsciously exert into making those people happy. Then, on the other hand, I want you to simply consider two commandments that Jesus gave. One commandment was to love the Lord your God with all your heart, mind, body, and soul. The other was to love your brother as yourself. Now think about how much time and energy you exert into those two commandments. Is it an equal effort, or is one area getting more attention than the other? If you are not exerting the majority of your effort into those two simple commandments that Jesus gave, then I must tell you that you are aggrieving God. If you are exerting more energy into pleasing others, don't be ashamed; you're not alone, and you will be free from this form of slavery. As long as you want to be free.

The next story is about a young girl by the name of Lisa. Lisa was a sophomore in high school. Lisa came from a middle-class family in which she lived with her mother, father, and younger brother. Lisa's mother loved God and served her church faithfully. Lisa's father was an atheist who worked hard, and Lisa was the apple of his eye. In her father's eyes, Lisa could do no wrong. In school Lisa hung out with one girl. Lisa's one friend's name was Amy. Amy was extremely outgoing while Lisa was an introvert. Amy smoked, but Lisa was a Christian. Amy dated boys on a regular basis while Lisa simply had a crush on one young man. Even though Lisa was young, she loved God.

Even though Lisa didn't understand a lot of things about God, she was infatuated with his creative ability and absolutely adored the story told in John 3:16. However, she had no one to talk to about that love. Amy loved smoking, boys, music, and TV shows that were flooded with sexuality and profanity and living the fast life. But Amy also loved Lisa. In Amy's eyes, Lisa was beautiful and intelligent, purely a leader. Lisa was everything that Amy wanted to be on the inside, but because Lisa didn't see herself as she truly was, her humility made Amy feel like she was the superstar. Lisa, on the other hand, absolutely idolized Amy. Amy was tall with long hair and had a beautiful face. Amy was funny and outgoing, and Lisa loved everything about her.

Lisa carried around this love for Jesus, yet because of Amy's behavior, Lisa was ashamed to talk about it. Lisa pretended to only have the same interests that Amy had. Lisa had a crush on the pastor's son at her church and saw him as perfect, but in school Lisa only showed attention to the exact same boys that Amy liked. Amy and Lisa always partied together, and during these parties, Lisa had been offered drugs, yet Lisa refused to partake up to this point. So, at this one particular party which took place during the week of Halloween, Lisa and Amy were joined by several of the boys and girls from their high school at an abandoned barn. There was loud music, alcohol, marijuana, and pills. Everyone was having a great time. Everyone was smiling and dancing. Lisa somehow lost sight of Amy and began to panic. When Lisa found Amy, she was behind a few bales of hay with two boys. Lisa froze and, for the first time in her life, heard the voice of God. Everything around her began to move in slow motion and the music was drowned out by this powerful yet subtle voice.

And the voice said, "This music, this alcohol, these drugs, and even your best friend are being used right now to usher you all directly to hell."

The voice continued, "If I were to come back right now, not one of you children would have a chance at salvation in this moment. Your mother prays for you daily and her prayers cover you at all times. Before I formed you in her womb, I knew you and I set you aside for a purpose and that purpose was not for you to follow Amy on the road to hell but rather for you to lead all of these children back to Me. From this moment on, you will be proud to be called My daughter, and I will use you as a light to lead my children from darkness back unto Me."

Lisa felt a sensation similar to cold chills and goosebumps, and she could not control the crying. She knew that God was right there with her, and she knew that she was not supposed to be there. She walked out of that party and no one tried to stop her.

As Lisa was walking, she suddenly heard the voice of God instruct her to go back, bring Amy home, and to not take no for an answer. Lisa immediately ran back inside to find Amy alone, and the two boys were trying to remove Amy's clothes. That night Amy had taken marijuana and two pills. Amy was barely conscious and fully unaware of what was being done to her. The two boys were furious and yelled at Lisa, "Leave her alone, this is what Amy wants."

Lisa replied, "If this is where she wants to be, she will tell me."

Amy reached out her hand very weakly and whispered the words, "Take me home Lisa, please take me home."

The two boys continued to argue with Lisa until she pulled out her cell phone and strongly warned them, "If you do not back off, I will have the police here in no time." The two boys backed off. Lisa walked Amy home and placed her in bed.

The next day Lisa came by to check on Amy. Amy didn't remember much about the night before. There was another party going on that night, and Amy began to talk about preparing for the next party. Lisa boldly interrupted her and told her that the night before she had heard the voice of God for the first time in her life. If it had not been for the voice of God, then Amy would have been raped by those two boys. Lisa told Amy that she loved her as a friend, but she loved God more. She told Amy that she was making the decision to stop following her and to stop idolizing her.

"Idolizing me?" replied Amy. "That's silly. You and I are best friends, and if anything, I idolize you."

Lisa said, "I'm not free to be myself around you, and all I do is follow you around attempting to be like you and make you happy, while in reality I'm not happy."

Amy asked, "Well, who are you?"

Lisa replied, "I am a child of God, and I love Jesus. I am not perfect, but I am not interested in music that demoralizes me. I am not interested in smoking and doing drugs. I am not interested in having sex with every guy that shows interest in me. I'm not claiming to be better than anyone, but I know my worth. I am a Christian And I will no longer hide in public, but on the contrary, I will proudly and boldly admit to anyone at any time that my faith is in God and I love Him first."

Amy began to cry, and she couldn't even reply. She was at a loss for words. As she sat there in silence Lisa walked over, wrapped her arms around her, and whispered in her ear, "God loves you too."

Amy replied, "Well how can I be a Christian too?"

The two began laughing and giggling like two little schoolgirls hysterically.

"It's easy silly," replied Lisa. Lisa led Amy into the Lord's prayer, and Amy accepted Jesus on a Saturday morning in her bedroom with her best friend. Suddenly, there was a knock at the door and the two girls ran downstairs to see who it was. Behold, it was the two boys from the party the night before.

Both of their faces were red as Lisa lashed out, yelling, "What the heck are you two doing here? I should call the police right now."

The two boys dropped to their knees and begged Amy for her forgiveness, yet Amy had no clue what they were repenting for. All she knew was that she had just accepted Jesus upstairs, and that it felt great. She was so full of excitement that she began to tell the boys, "Hey, I just accepted Jesus, and it feels great. My heart feels brand new and the feeling that I have on the inside can't be explained. You should do it too, you need this. Right, Lisa, they need this?"

Lisa was still angry, but the voice of the Spirit gently instructed Lisa to form a circle with Amy and the two boys and lead them into prayer.

"For everything that happened the night before was designed to lead these three children up to this very moment," said the Spirit. Lisa led them into the Lord's prayer, and the two boys accepted Christ in Amy's living room on a Saturday morning after the night they almost raped a young girl. The adversary had a plan for them to throw away their lives while ruining Amy's life. God sent a way of escape! Lisa was no longer a slave to pleasing Amy, and Amy found freedom from her sins. The two boys were delivered in the process.

Now sit back and imagine how the story would have ended if Lisa hadn't been obedient? What would have happened to Amy and those two boys if Lisa had ignored that voice and kept drinking or taking drugs rather than leave? The answer is that the adversary would have won, and the consequences for these sins would have fell on the heads of these four children. But thanks to Lisa having been obedient to the voice of God, not only was she set free, but she led three others to freedom in less than twenty-four hours.

You are as bold as Lisa. Take a stand for the King of Kings. Don't be afraid to be who you are. Don't be afraid to speak up about right and wrong around your friends. You no longer have to live in the shadows of your friends or family. Christ has set you free, so live in that freedom and lead others to the same freedom that was given to you.

Slave to Righteousness

The goal of all Christians is to become slaves of righteousness. The only way to break the chains that keep us bound in sin is to (1) accept Jesus as our Lord and Savior, and (2) allow Him to lead us out of captivity and into eternal life. You can accomplish this by praying daily, reading His Word, and joining a spirit-filled church.

When you are a slave to things like fear, money, sex, and pleasing others, this sinful nature is displeasing to God. You find yourself living a life that is actually a facade. You find yourself living a life that is full of pain and regrets. You find yourself living a life that isn't fulfilling, leaving you with a void that is often filled with drugs, alcohol, or some sort of self-fulfilling yet self-destructive mechanism. The only alternative to remaining in the slavery of sin is to fully submit to Christ and yield yourself to His way of life which leads to becoming a slave of righteousness.

Imagine being free in a way in which you had no care nor thought about what other people thought about you. Imagine being free from cigarettes and not worrying about dying from cancer. Imagine being free from marijuana, heroin, cocaine, or crystal meth. Imagine being free from worrying about contracting HIV and other STDs. Imagine being free from all of your fears. No, not one of your fears, but all of your fears? The only one you should fear is God alone. Yet many of us have a list of fears a mile long. Right now, I'm going to show you how we can turn these imaginations into reality with this simple formula.

The freedom formula:

Accept Jesus + study God's word + apply God's word = freedom.

Step One: accepting Jesus. Accepting Jesus is the first step to obtaining your freedom. John 14:6 (NKJV) states that Jesus is the way, the truth, and the light, and no one comes to the Father except through Him. The beautiful part is that you can do this anywhere. You can accept Jesus in the presence of your congregation at church, or you can accept Jesus all alone in your car during lunch break. Jesus is everywhere, and He never sleeps nor slumbers. Jesus is like that concerned father waiting at the door for His child to come home. Jesus is like that last watchman walking back and forth in front of the gate, waiting for those last couple stragglers to get home before the door shuts.

Jesus is like that diligent lifeguard watching the waves, waiting for someone to call His name so that He can enter the waters and grab your hand before you drown. There is no convenient time, and there is no perfect place. The best time is right now, and the best place is exactly where you are. There is no need to think or say, "I have to get myself together before I can accept Jesus." If you think that way you will be waiting forever. Jesus is prepared to accept you exactly the way you are. The Bible says that a sin is sin, meaning no sin is greater than the other. The Bible also clearly says that all men have sinned and fallen short of the glory of God. That means that even your pastor has sinned. Even I have sinned. Therefore, none of us are better or worse than you.

God loves you exactly the way you are, and Jesus is prepared to usher you into the presence of the father if you would only accept Him. Don't overthink it and don't allow your mind to overtake you with thoughts of why it won't work. I'm living proof that it does work, and I know lots of people who it has worked for. Now is the time for you to let it work for you. Repeat these words if you're ready now:

Jesus, I believe that You are the Son of God, and I believe that You gave Your life for me. Jesus, I believe that You are the way, the truth, and the light, and I ask that You enter my heart. Jesus, I ask that You would be my King and sit on the throne of my heart now and forever. Jesus, I love You and I thank You for being my King, Amen.

And just like that, you have accepted Christ! You are saved. You are a Christian! You are now a child of the Living God. Everything is not going to change overnight, and everything is not going to get better overnight. But you are free.

The next step is to study God's Word. I want you to download the Bible app on your phone and find a translation that works for you. I recommend the NKJV, NIV, or NLT translations for new believers, but there are many different translations. Please find the translation that is best for you. Every day, I want you to set aside some time just to study God's Word. I also recommend starting out with the book of Genesis in the first chapter. The book of Genesis beautifully displays God's creative abilities. The entire book of Genesis is a synopsis of the entire Bible. Genesis will teach you about the common problems that we all have as human beings. We have a God who has given us everything we would ever need, but He also gave us free choice.

Sometimes our free choice and the influence of our adversary leads us to make decisions that grieve God. The consequence of sin is death. Death is not always a physical death, but it can also be spiritual and emotional. Genesis tells the story of how people are sometimes selfish and take/do what is forbidden. As a result, we fall. God, being wise and all-knowing, has always provided a way for us to be redeemed back to Him. The blood of His Son redeemed us, and this is how you gain your freedom. Christ set the captives free. Yes, the captives include you and me!

The Bible has a way of opening our minds. The truth that is written in this divine book holds all the keys that you will ever need to overcome your fears, your addictions, and whatever else that has you bound in sin. So how long will it take to obtain my freedom you may ask? The answer to that question is entirely up to you. In the book of Exodus, you will read about the children of Israel and how they were delivered from Egypt. Egypt symbolizes sin. God delivers Israel and His people from sin and promises them a new territory where they would be free and prosperous. God begins to lead them out of captivity. The Bible says that the journey was only a forty-day trip, but because Israel was disobedient, had poor attitudes, and often failed to follow the instructions given by God, the trip ended up taking forty years. So just like the children of Israel, you have control over the length of your trip. Your trip to freedom could take you a couple days or it could take you a couple years. It all depends on you and your obedience. It depends on how bad you truly want to be free.

Let's examine Romans 6:12-13 (NKJV). It reads:

> Therefore do not let sin reign in your mortal body, that you should obey it in its lust. And do not present your members as instruments of unrighteousness to sin but present yourselves to God as being alive from the dead and your members as instruments of righteousness to God. For sin shall not have dominion over you!
>
> –Romans 6:12-13, NKJV

So basically, these verses are saying to no longer position yourself to simply satisfy the needs of your flesh, body, and sinful nature. Instead, position yourself to satisfy God and allow Him to use you as an instrument. You are no longer a slave to sin!

Take a drug dealer who is talented at selling and managing money. He puts aside his desire to destroy his community by making a fast dollar, and he instead uses his skills working for a local retailer. With God's favor, he climbs from a floor salesman to the department manager. He is using his gift to earn a living in a way that glorifies God, and he is no longer part of a system that destroys God's people. Simple change, big impact. Let us set aside our sinful nature and use our gifts in ways that glorify God. We are no longer slaves to sin, but instead we are slaves to God.

The third and final step is to apply God's Word and practice it consistently. Read James 1:21-22 (NKJV), which states, "Therefore, lay aside all filthiness and overflow of wickedness and receive with meekness the implanted word, which is able to save your souls. But be doers of the word, and not hearers only." So, we have put away all of the sins and behaviors that don't please God. We are reading His Word and implanting it into our hearts as it saves our souls and changes our lives. But we can't make the mistake of just reading the Word, we must do what it tells us, or we won't reap the benefits. Lots of people know the Word of God and can quote it, but only a select few actually act according to what's written in it. Even I still have a lot of work to do in this area.

Start with the basics. All of the commandments can be summed up in the two that Jesus referred to.

1. Love the Lord your God with all your heart. If you love God, you will spend time with Him in prayer and in His word. If you love God, you won't put idols like money, other people, or bad habits before Him. If you love Him, God will come first, and you will honor Him in all that you do. This doesn't mean that you won't make mistakes. But your love for God and your commitment to Him won't allow you to make the same mistakes over and over again.
2. Love your neighbor as yourself. All men were created in the image of God. If you love God, you must love His most prized creations, PEOPLE. Neighbors are any and everybody in this world. We are instructed to love our neighbors, as we love ourselves. Sinning against other people is hard to do when we love them with the love of Christ. Not reacting to people in need is hard to do when we love our neighbors with the love of Christ.

If you can simply abide by these two commandments, everything else will fall into place. There are a lot of do's and don'ts in the Bible, so just focus on these two rules for now.

Another characteristic that I want you to act on in boldness. Read the entire book of Joshua. It's my favorite book for a new believer. Joshua was a new leader, and he was instructed to learn the law of the Lord (His Word) and to meditate on it. God told Him that if He followed these simple instructions and remained strong and courageous, God would never leave Him or forsake Him. That promise is true for us also. Study His Word, meditate on it daily, act upon His Word, and you can't fail. This doesn't mean that we won't have minor setbacks, but as long as God is for us, who can be against us? Be courageous and strong. Be confident but not arrogant. Feel confident in the fact that God loves you and rescued you from a life of bondage.

Be confident in the fact that you are no longer a slave. God has set you free and granted you eternal life. God's promises are a "yes" and an "Amen" to those who love Him. Remain obedient to God and position yourself as a servant. Don't be like the people who only want to take. Instead, be a servant who always gives thanks to their Father, even when things don't go their way. My favorite scripture of the Bible was also my grandmother's: Psalm 1. This is my goal for my life. This can be the goal for your life also.

> Blessed is the man who walks not in the counsel of the ungodly, nor stands in the path of sinners, nor sits in the seat of scornful; but his delight is in the law of the Lord, and in His law, he meditates day and night. He shall be like a tree planted by the rivers of water that brings forth its fruit in its season, whose leaf shall not wither. And whatever he does shall prosper. The ungodly are not so but are like the chaff that the wind drives away.
>
> –Psalm 1, NKJV

David wrote this psalm while he was a living witness to the favor of God. The psalm states that anyone who is a slave to righteousness and meditates daily on God's Word would prosper. You can have God's favor and yield your fruit if you live according to this scripture.

Lastly my brothers and sisters, reflect on Jeremiah 18. It's a beautiful story about how God is the potter, and we are the clay.

No matter how broken or damaged you appear to be, God can still mold you into a beautiful vessel. I was once a porn addicted, money-hungry, drug dealer. But now I am a Christian, a father, a husband, a CEO, and an author. I was once a broken vessel, but I gave myself to the Potter, and now he is using my gift of writing to pour into your life. Will you join me in this life of freedom and abundance? Will you tell your neighbors about God? Will you give this book to the next slave who's ready to be set free? Please do. Please join me. Follow me as I follow Christ, and let's free our brothers and sisters.

> I can do all things through Christ who strengthens me. With God you can and will overcome anything that your mind can conceive.
>
> --Philippians 4:13, NKJV

Closing Remarks

God implanted this book in my heart back in 2005. God has a strong desire for His children to return home back to Him. The enemy controls the majority of the people here on Earth. He is controlling young and old through fear, the lust of the flesh, the lust of the eyes, and the pride of life. All of these sins and fears have been present in the hearts of men since the fall of man in the garden of Eden. Read Genesis for yourself. Don't depend on a preacher, read it for yourself. The enemy, Satan, has been using the same tricks since the beginning of time. One of his latest devices of manipulation and deceit is to make people think that he doesn't exist. That's what Satan wants people to believe, that neither him nor hell exists.

Satan wants people to believe that he doesn't exist. I once read about warriors who were outnumbered by their opponents, but they had a brilliant strategy and were therefore effective killing machines. These warriors would camouflage themselves in the bushes and even underground. When their opponents got close enough, the warriors would strike and kill soldiers by the hundreds. Satan is using the same strategy. He wants people to believe that he doesn't exist while he wreaks havoc on the earth. Some people say that ignorance is bliss. Don't be deceived. Satan is real, and his mission is to steal, kill, and destroy us.

Read Revelation 12. It describes how Satan and one third of the angels were cast to the earth after a holy war. The Bible says in Revelation 12:12 (NKJV), "Woe unto the people of the people of the earth because the devil was thrown down with great wrath and he knows that his time is short." Satan's desire was to be exalted on high like God. But God makes it clear that those who exalt themselves will be humbled. Satan's plan is not only to lead as many souls to hell as possible but also to control the majority of the population here on earth. He torments people with fear. He leads people away from God by feeding their egos. He puts thoughts into our minds in such a way that we often believe they are our own thoughts. Satan is a master at subtlety. So many are being subdued by his devices yet don't even realize it.

No Longer A Slave is a wake-up call for every community in the world. Drug addiction, sexual sin, and trading our lives and freedom for money is not the norm. Being a slave to maintaining standards set by culture and the media is not the norm. You can be free in Christ. You can be free to live happy with yourself, just the way you are. We can be free to admit that we believe in God openly. We can be free to admit that we love Jesus openly. This book will set millions of captives free. This book, along with the Spirit of God, will open the eyes of children and adults around the world. This book is designed to be bring God's children home, and that's what it will do until the end of time.

Will you help me set the captives free? If the answer is yes, here is how. Give this book away after you read it. Don't keep this book on shelf. What good is a key on a shelf when millions are chained and bound? If you can buy more copies and give those away, please do so also. Tell people about the goodness of God and boldly proclaim His goodness every chance you get. And lastly, pray for your community. Pray for the lost, the orphans, and the widows. If you have means to give to them, by all means, give to them as well. If we all do a little, overall, we will accomplish a lot.

Thanks for reading,
Allandis Russ

CPSIA information can be obtained
at www.ICGtesting.com
Printed in the USA
LVHW020547040121
675399LV00007B/949

9 781647 736200